To M ,

Many thanks for
your wonderful
contribution to my
book.

With love &
man hugs!

Tony
x

26.8.16.

ISBN: 978-0-9956049-0-2

Cover design by Sammy Blindell
Illustrations by Jennifer Garrity
Edited by Kym Ciftci

The Publisher has used  its best endeavours to ensure that any website addresses referred to in this book are correct and active  at the time of going to press. However, the publisher and the author have no responsibility whatsoever for the websites  and can make no guarantee  that a site will remain live or that  the content will remain relevant, pertinent or appropriate.

"Your perfect partner is not an idealistic vision or flawless fantasy,
but rather someone who supports you in your purpose
and fulfilment of your destiny
– as you do in theirs."


Tony Brown

For anyone who has ever thought…

"Where on Earth is *my* perfect partner?"

# CONTENTS

# **FOREWORD**

Many people fall into an intimate relationship with another person simply because of that biological imperative (lust); and, many other people end up as a couple because of the cultural programming that tells us that is how one's life is supposed to unfold - married with kids, a job and an assigned role in society.

As a consequence, many relationships devolve into unsatisfying and unfulfilling periods of equilibrium and then entropy. They fall apart. Other relationships become codependent. Neither partner is fulfilled in the relationship but the other at least provides a sense of belonging and a bastion against loneliness.

Of course, many of these relationships that come about in the normal course of things evolve into mature love and/or develop into long term friendships filled with compassion and understanding. Couples change and grow together, creating a shared life of building a relationship, a family and a way to navigate into the future together.

There is however, for some, a special kind of relationship in which each partner reflects the sacredness of the other. The other does not just exist to fulfill some need or lack; to be not only a mirror reflecting one's own beauty, but to be a channel for the soul's longing to fully and freely love.

Deep down, we all feel that this profound type of love is available; that this special person is out there in the world somewhere. Maybe they are even actively looking for you right now.

In this book, Tony Brown details his own journey to the realisation of that one relationship that so many long to have - the encounter with the perfect partner, their soulmate.

If you are still looking for that perfect relationship with a loving partner, or if you are already in a relationship that you would like to enhance, this book will answer the question... 'How do I find or attract my soulmate?' And, it will also, I believe, empower you to become the soulmate of the person you may already be in a loving relationship with.

All our relationships are mirrors that give us the opportunity for self-examination and self-realisation. The process that Tony details herein is that and more. I believe you will discover that your relationship with this book will be both rewarding and empowering.

And finally, and perhaps most germane of all, if you follow along as Tony explains how to find your soulmate, you will also discover how to develop the most important relationship of all... the one with yourself.

*Leslie Fieger*

*Author of The Delfin Trilogy*

# ABOUT THE AUTHOR

What Tony Brown has done, is what most of us have to do; make our own way in life and learn the lessons as we go.

As he strived to be lucky in life, Tony always seemed to be unlucky in love. Why? What was he doing wrong? Whilst he spent forty years learning lessons in love, it was the creation of his winning formula that finally made finding his soulmate a reality. And it all started in the unlikeliest of places…

Tony's passion for sports cars and motorsport had fuelled an ambition to become a racing driver. Whilst he describes the adrenaline charged world of motorsport as exhilarating, addictive and expensive, his fun ended with the realisation that the only prize he was ever going to win, was first place at the Bank for the biggest overdraft! Not long after, both Tony's professional and personal lives were also doomed to go the way of his racing exploits . . . bust.

Deep in debt, divorced for the second time and facing bankruptcy, he puzzled as to why it is that some people seem to possess a phenomenal ability to achieve, do and have more. So he thought it was about time he focussed on improving his understanding of what it is that successful people actually *do*. And so he immersed himself in the field of human and personal potential.

Tony took all the lessons learned, condensed them into a simple, step-by-step formula (one he still uses to this day) and applied them to his own life with remarkable results. Income doubled, trebled, then quadrupled and he knew his professional life was back on track as his Bank Manager was speaking to him again!

## Testing Times

There was still the matter of unfinished business in the world of motor racing to attend to. Only this time his approach was to *really* test his formula for success by competing in the highest subscribed, one-make race series in Europe. A Porsche Championship with identical, equally matched cars and closely regulated, so that no one could gain an advantage on their fellow competitors.

So far, in his somewhat mediocre racing career, Tony had never qualified anywhere near the front of the field, led a race nor been on the podium. He hadn't won a thing. Well, apart from that prize at the Bank of course. His motor racing statistics to date made woeful reading: Races 27. Pole positions, fastest laps, podium finishes and race wins; 0.

Graded as a novice, Tony entered the first race of the season - against 37 other experienced racers. The difference this time, was that he was armed with his own formula for success and functioning at new heights of self-awareness, belief and understanding.

# Racing Success

The sequence of events that took place on that day and after it, were astonishing. Tony not only qualified his car in pole position, ahead of the field, but also led the race, set the fastest lap time and won! Subsequently, in the first seven races of that year he led all seven races, won five and broke a lap record, which had stood for six years.

Naturally, all of this raised a few eyebrows in the pit lane and a fellow competitor asked Tony what he attributed his new-found success to. At the time of course, he was not going to reveal his winning formula or 'secret' to anyone, especially a fellow competitor! Later that year, Tony sealed his success by being crowned as championship winner.

Since utilising his winning formula, Tony has competed in a total of five championship campaigns, been the championship winner three times and a close runner-up twice. His race stats since, now make for very different reading: Races 136. Pole positions 47. Fastest laps 36. Podiums 95. Races wins 40.

# Unlucky in Love

Appearing or pretending to be successful on the outside is one thing, but actually *being* successful on the inside is another. As Tony now found himself divorced for the *third* time, he wondered why his relationships always seemed great in the beginning, but then never went the distance.

It was a friend's passing comment that made him re-evaluate everything he *really* wanted from lasting love, and it was then he had that light-bulb moment. If his winning formula worked so well in business *and* in his motor racing life, then why wouldn't it work for his love life too?

Just as he set the bar high when he returned to racing, he would do so again when looking for his true love. The reward this time would be to find his soulmate, the person he is here and *meant* to be with.

## The Winning Formula

Tony made some relevant adjustments to his formula and went about finding his perfect partner. The rest, as they say, is history, and now he shares all of his secrets in this book, for you. Whilst a fellow competitor missed out on Tony's winning ways, *you* will not. Here he explains what and what not to do, along with all the reasons why the things we do work, or more importantly, don't. His process is one that's simple, easy to follow and one that anyone can do.

As he says: *"What's been better than making money or racing fast cars, has been applying this winning formula to my love life and finding my soulmate - the person I'm here and meant to be with".*

Tony now spends his time sharing, teaching and coaching his winning formula, to those who truly desire to find their perfect partner too.

'We gain the strength
of the temptation
we resist'

Ralph Waldo Emerson

# **TEMPTATION**

## (PREFACE)

We've all been in a relationship of one kind or another, that's why we all have an opinion of what works and what doesn't. What to do and what not to do. What's right and what's wrong. So it's easy to offer advice to others about the topic, as we call upon our own experiences, both good and bad.

Can you think of a time when someone has sought your advice about their relationship issue? Likewise, have others ever given you their advice about yours; whether you sought it or not? We all have some experience to call upon and an opinion to hand when it comes to matters of the heart.

Then surely it follows that as we all have some experience of relationships (granted some more than others), that we're all now hooked up with our respective perfect partners and living happily ever after too, right? No? If not, then why not?...

• What is stopping your perfect partner from finding you?

• What's preventing you from finding them?

- Why are they so elusive?

- How do we break this cycle of either luckless searching or repeated break-ups?

## All The Good Ones Are Taken!

Yes I know it's all too easy to say 'all the good ones are taken', but saying that is just, at best a cop-out and at worst frustration. The grass always *looks* greener on the other side and we all want what we can't have. Moreover, today's fast paced, technologically driven world commands that we can access an instant answer to any question. So why is it then that the answers to the above questions are so difficult to find?

Hence the purpose of this book is to not only share with you the often hidden, subconscious mistakes that we sometimes make, but to help you shine a light on your path so that your perfect partner can find you too.

This book explains the strategies that work and most of all, how to utilise the universal laws of attraction to your complete advantage. These are the same procedures that have helped me and others find their soulmates, and they can do the same for you too. You can find the person you are here and *meant* to be with.

The wish to find our perfect partner, our soulmate, is one of the most powerful human desires there is. That is, to be in the right relationship with the right person, at the right time. The person who is absolutely perfect for you, as you are for them. But how exactly do you find them and how can they find you?

# The Reason

Firstly, it's important to recognise that people don't just come into our lives by accident or coincidence. I'm sure you've heard that there is no such thing as a coincidence? If this is the case, then there's a reason; a purpose behind meeting someone, the things they say and do and the actions we take as a result. And there could be any one of several objectives behind this.

It could be that there's a lesson for us to learn, or perhaps some guidance or direction that's needed at the right time. Have you ever reflected and come to realise that someone has taught you a life lesson, either good or bad? Or that if it wasn't for them, you'd never have learnt it? Have you ever gone through a painful experience and been completely demoralised, disheartened and dismayed as to the purpose of ever meeting that person? Only to reflect upon it at a later date and then understood the real reason behind it?...

The boss you dislike because they fired you. Only for you to realise that if they hadn't done that, you would never have found the better job and career path you have now.

Similarly, it could be that someone crossed your path and inspired you to take some form of action that you otherwise may not have taken. Or, because of them, you became more courageous and bold as a result of their input. Of course, it could have been for you to learn some lessons in love too…

The lover who possibly jilted you and broke your heart, only for you to later recognise that actually, it *was* for the best and had they not done so, then you'd never be with the person you're with now.

Whatever the circumstances, we should be most grateful to anyone who comes into our lives and for the lessons learnt, both good and bad. If it wasn't for them, then you wouldn't be the wonderful person you are today.

So, given that there's a reason for people to come into our lives and that their presence doesn't happen by accident or coincidence, then it follows that we have the ability to attract who we want, or need, for any particular circumstance or situation that befalls us. After all, we're attracting them already, albeit on an *unconscious* basis. All we need to do now is simply bring it into our conscious awareness.

## The Answer

So how *do* we attract the one person who is absolutely right for us? Our perfect partner and soulmate.

Well, it sounds simple, but all we need to do is cease any pretence, shine a light on our true self and start to walk our true path. Then our perfect partner can find us. So how do we do that exactly?

As we all know, a question is easy if you already know the answer. Believe me, there would be nothing I would like more than to just say, go to page 'x', paragraph 'y', line 'z' and the answer you've been looking for is there. But this subject matter doesn't work like that because, well, it's subjective.

So I implore you to resist temptation and not simply jump to the end of this book (if you've not already done so) in your quest for instant gratification. Believe me, it won't work because it's been written in such a way, that each chapter builds upon the previous. Therefore I assure you, leaping to the end will not provide you with any instant answers.

# The Results

Instead, take your time and be honest with yourself along the way. The truer you are to yourself in this process, the more you will gain from these pages.

In my journey, I have discovered that there are ten potential reasons why our perfect partner can't find us. Amongst them is at least one that will be applicable to you... I guarantee it. So there is much to be gained here. Therefore, you are now holding in your hands a very powerful tool that you can utilise to your complete advantage. One that can change your future and your destiny as to who you are meant to be with.

Our time here doesn't have to be hard work or spent alone. We all deserve to lead a life full of fun, happiness and success with the person we're meant to be with. And being part of a truly loving, respectful and fulfilling relationship with your soulmate, beats anything else in life into a distant second place.

And with my track record, believe me if I can do it, anyone can!

Enjoy your journey. It is most definitely worth it.

Tony Brown

# TEMPTATION
In a nutshell:

## 'It is difficult to be patient, but to waste the reward for patience is worse.'

Abu Bakr

'If we could all sell
our experiences for what
they cost us, we'd all be
millionaires.'

Abigail Van Buren

# 1

# THE COST

You could be holding this book in your hands for any number of reasons; Perhaps you're a bit tired and fed up of attracting the wrong type of person into your life? Or maybe the traditional forms of dating are simply not working for you. Could it be that you're uncomfortable with the apparent need to be out every Friday and Saturday night? You know, trawling the pubs and clubs in the hope that your ideal match will fall directly into your lap. And if they do, that they're not too drunk!

Maybe you've tried online dating too and that hasn't worked either. Or the whole concept of being online simply doesn't sit right with you in the first place. Perhaps you've just come out of a relationship and you're feeling a little daunted, as things have changed a lot since you were last on the dating scene.

Possibly you're still *in* a relationship, but that relationship no longer serves you. And you may be putting a brave face on it, but you know there will come a time when enough will be enough and being on your own will be far better than staying with the wrong person.

Whatever the reason, deep down you probably feel that you really do desire and deserve to be with the *right* partner. And in doing so, living your life within a truly loving and fulfilling relationship. At least I hope you do.

## Imagine

So imagine then, being with someone who not only likes all the things that you do, but that together, you complement each other in such a way that life itself takes on a whole new meaning. Problems seem to pale into insignificance and life just seems a whole lot easier. It's like driving a car when all the traffic lights are green; life just flows much more easily.

Picture being out with friends and they come up to you and say: "Wow! What you guys have together is amazing. I wish my relationship was like that. Where did you meet? What did you do? What did you say?" They will want to know and want what you have.

Imagine being with someone who respects you completely for who you really are. And you're so in tune with each other, that you both recognise you're here to support one another in what you're here to do.

So the question is, if you want to go from being or feeling on your own, to that of sharing your life with the person you're *meant* to be with, then I'm sure you'd agree that you may need a slightly different approach to those you've tried thus far. That's what this book is about; to share with you how you can find the person who is perfect for you.

Now I know what you're thinking; there's no such thing as a 'perfect person'. But I believe, in fact I know, there is such a thing as being able to find the person who is perfect for *you*.

## The Price of Love

Whilst the benefits of finding your perfect partner may be obvious and you can't put a price on true love, it seems that today you can put a price on finding it.

Recent research has calculated that the average cost of going on a date in the UK, when you factor everything in, is £127 (each). Further research states that it takes us on average, thirteen dates (seven of which are complete disasters) and eighteen months before we find the partner we believe to be 'the one'.

I'm sure you would agree with me that it shouldn't really be a numbers game or about dating anybody and everybody. But at least we've now found 'the one' and we're now past the post as it were. Happy days!

Research goes on to say that we then spend the next twelve months and a further £3,629 dating our new love, followed by a further £2,760 in the second year, before we realise in year three that the relationship isn't right. Yes, that's correct. The average length of time we stay in a relationship today in the UK, is just two years and nine months. The 'seven year itch' it seems, has been reduced to less than half in these modern times.

So, that's an investment of more than four years and well over £8,000 and you're now back to square one!

But here's the thing. When you know who you are and therefore, what would be perfect for you, you don't have to do all of that. How come? Because now you *know* exactly what you're looking for. This is where so many people go wrong. What most people do when searching for their next partner is to simply look at what's out there and what's available. When in actual fact, in order to find who's perfect for you, first you need to look inside, not outside.

What's the cost of not getting this right? Well, you could end up in a relationship that doesn't serve you, or a marriage that doesn't either. If you do, then you could end up as one of the 42% of marriages that end in divorce in the UK today. And the average cost of that is £44,000.

## The Real Cost

In situations like this, it's not about the money, nor is it about you or your partner. The real cost is in how it affects others around you.

You may have children in your life. They may not be your children; they could be nieces, nephews or other (associated) family members. As we all know, children are not stupid. Quite the opposite in fact. They are watching you and modelling themselves on you. What is it that you're teaching them? It's okay to stay in a relationship that doesn't serve you? Or that you deserve to live a life of fun, happiness and success with the person you're meant to be with? Do you want these children to look up to you or to look away?

And why is *now* so important? Well, how many more years and £8,000+ do you want to be spending with the wrong people? Surely you'd rather be investing you're time and money with the person who is going to be in your life long term?

And why the heck listen to me and what I have to say on the subject? Well, before we begin our journey together, allow me to explain how I came to be writing about a subject that's so close to all our hearts.

# THE COST
### In a nutshell:

## 'The price of anything is the amount of life you exchange for it.'

Henry David Thoreau

'There's a difference
between who we love,
who we settle with and
who we're meant for'

Kevin Hart

# 2

# MEANT TO BE

It's September 2006 and after twelve years together, you find me separating from my third wife, young son and teenager stepdaughter. So much for third time lucky then!

I'd like to say that this is where my journey started, but the reality is that it started over thirty years previously when, like most teenagers, I started dating without any instruction manual, lessons or advice. I ended up going from one relationship to the next, not knowing what I wanted, or what I was looking for. As my experience grew, I only seemed to know what it was that I didn't want and sometimes, I attracted exactly that!

However, two years on from this separation and subsequent third divorce, you now find me making yet another fresh start as I move into my new home. It's ideal for me; a lovely Georgian styled, three-storey town house. It's nestled in a row of seven amongst tendered gardens and set in a peaceful part of town, yet only a fifteen-minute walk to the beach.

# Wise Wendy

My friend Wendy has just popped round. Wendy is an attractive lady in her late forties, 5' 4" with long blonde hair and she's married to my good friend Pete. I call her 'Wise Wendy' as she's always coming out with pearls of wisdom.

"Hi Tony, I just thought I'd drop by and give you a little house warming gift from the both of us."

A kind and thoughtful gesture that gives her the perfect excuse to see inside my new pad.

"Thanks Wendy." I say.

I know her curiosity has been getting the better of her, so I duly give her the grand tour of my new abode.

Wendy clearly approves of my new surroundings, but it's also clear that she's short on time and quickly heads back to the front door. Looking slightly puzzled she says;

"I love your house. It's so perfect for you. But where's Suzi, your girlfriend? We haven't seen her for a while."

A little embarrassed I replied "Oh, well, ummm... I've just ended that. It wasn't going anywhere."

"Oh. Isn't that just what you said about Mandy, Jane and who was the other one . . . Lisa? I'd have thought that you being a racing driver and running a successful business, that it would be easy for you to find the right woman. Maybe you're meant to be on your own and this is just going to be a bachelor pad. Anyway, sorry I can't stop, we'll see you soon. Bye."

And with that she was gone.

Have you ever had a time in your life when someone has said something in passing that has shaken, stunned or rocked you to your core? A wake-up call if you will.

Her words "...maybe you're meant to be on your own..." stopped me dead in my tracks.

Okay, so how do I feel about that? It feels fine and sits well with me. I live on my own now and I've been on my own before, but I'd never thought of it in that way; that I'm *meant* to be on my own. As if it's my destiny. Actually that would make a lot of sense as to why I can't seem to find the person who is right for me. Well I'm not prepared to just be in any relationship for the sake of it that's for sure.

That day I made a decision; I am either going to be on my own, *or* I will be with the person who I'm meant to be with.

Now, I'd like to tell you that having made that decision, I knew exactly what to do and my perfect partner turned up on my doorstep the very next day. But we all know that life doesn't work like that, does it. Life is more like a roller coaster, full of highs and lows and ups and downs.

So, I spent the following years researching and finding out which dating strategies work, which don't and which ones are supposed to work, but don't. I learnt what to do and what not to do. I read everything I could lay my hands on and put into practise all the advice the world had to offer - you name it, I did it.

# Comic Keith

You now find me in 2014, at my local pub and out for a drink with my mate of some 40 years, Keith. We originally met at the age of 16 when we started our Apprenticeship together. I call him Comic Keith as he's always joking and like me, he's a bit of a petrol head. It's like having your own Jeremy Clarkson in the room when Keith's around.

"Tony, I've met most of your girlfriends, all of your wives and we've eaten a lot of wedding cake together. At one point I thought it was your favourite dish!"

I laugh, but he continued unabated…

"But I have to say, what you and Jeni have together is amazing. To be honest, when you said that you'd either be on your own or with the one you're meant to be with, I never thought you'd do it. But fair play, I've never seen you so happy. When did you know Jeni was the one?"

I knew the answer to that question in a heartbeat, so my response was instant.

"We both knew after about six weeks."

"Yeah, but Tony… *How* did you know?"

Ah, here's the real question behind the question and not the first time I've been asked this either. Why is it that everyone seems to want to know? So this time my response was a little more considered.

"I'll let you into a little secret… It's when you come to realise why it hasn't worked out with anyone else."

Keith hesitated, looked straight into my eyes and came back with;

"You should write a book. In fact, you should be in the business of helping others find their perfect partner too. Let's face it, you certainly have the experience and I reckon by showing others how you've done it, you could save people a lot of time, money and heartache."

Hmmm… Another one of those passing comments masquerading as a wake-up call? Share with others how I did it . . . how I found my perfect partner, my soulmate, the person I'm here and meant to be with? I reckon I could do that, in fact I'd love to do that!

So, as you can see, by the evidence you are holding in your hands . . . I wrote the book and I'm in the business of helping others find their perfect partner too.

Maybe third time wasn't so lucky for me, but I've come to realise that good things do actually come in threes; I'm a three times motor racing champion, I've taken three businesses from start up to success and I have three ex-wives!

However, I have now found a new lucky number. You see, I have found 'one'. The one thing that's better than racing fast cars or making money is being with the person that you're meant to be with.

Exactly how I achieved this, and how you can too, is revealed, in detail, in the following ten chapters. Ten possible reasons why your perfect partner can't find you…

# MEANT TO BE
### In a nutshell:

'The one thing that's better than racing fast cars or making money, is being with the person that you're meant to be with.'

Tony Brown

'If you don't believe in yourself, why should anybody else?'

Teresa Mummert

# 3

# **BELIEF**

## [Reason #1]

At the forefront of our journey, we need to be consciously aware of two topics. One we often have too much of and the other, not enough. First we will deal with the one that is all too often in short supply: 'Belief.'

It may sound a little silly, but first and foremost (and this is where most people go wrong), you have to truly believe that finding your perfect partner is completely possible. This *is* a fundamental principle for success in anything you choose to achieve in life. Firstly, you must believe it to receive it. So please, doubt your doubts before you doubt your beliefs!

Unfortunately, statistical research puts us in the minority here. I did say this is where *most* people go wrong. Research has revealed that, as much as 60% of singles in the UK had reached a point where they believed they were never going to find their perfect partner. If you feel that you too have reached that point, then let's just pause for a moment, take a deep breath and consider why this is so.

It would be far too easy for me to say that because your mind is already made up, there's little point in you continuing with this book and the process that lies ahead. The reason being is that you will just get to the end (if you get that far) and still believe that finding your perfect partner is not going to happen. And if you do that, guess what? It won't.

However, the good news is that you can have anything you want, if you're willing to give up the belief that you can't have it!

## Cognitive Dissonance

To this end, I know that once you understand and recognise how much a belief can cloud your view and judgement, then there will be complete justification in continuing. In other words, your mind will be open to receiving the content within this book and the wonderful future that's ahead of you. Particularly as we are talking about something as life changing as finding your soulmate.

Unfortunately, most people don't see their beliefs. Instead their beliefs *tell* them what to see. Furthermore, a truth they believe and adhere to makes them unavailable to see or hear anything new.

So, unless your state of belief has already been shifted, what you see will always depend on what you're looking for (what you already believe). This is crucial, because for those who do believe, no proof is necessary. For those who don't, no proof is possible. What this means is, if you believe it will happen, then you'll see the opportunities. If you believe it will not, then you'll see nothing but problems, obstacles and difficulties.

You however, are far too smart to be the only thing standing in your way. So here's how it works…

Sometimes you may hold a belief that is very strong, usually triggered by a highly emotional event, personal experience or a 'truth' that you were told when young. When you are presented with evidence that contradicts that belief, then you cannot accept it. Why not? Because it creates within you a feeling that is extremely uncomfortable (Cognitive Dissonance). Then, in the interests of pain avoidance, it naturally becomes important to protect that belief. Therefore you will not only begin a process of justification (defence), but also ignore and even deny any new information that does not sit comfortably with what you believe.

In other words, your mind could already (unconsciously) be made up. Yes, no doubt with very good reason. But now you know the psychology of how this process works, you are much better placed to allow your mind to be open and receptive. Excellent.

This in turn means that things, situations and chances will start to happen for you. This is why opportunities, accidents and coincidence don't just happen. You actually create them. Hence the saying; 'there's no such thing as a coincidence.'

## Good News!

Further good news is that researchers found 94% of women *do* believe in true love and 88% of men feel the same way. So whilst 60% may have reached a point in believing they're never going to find their perfect partner, an overwhelming majority still hold a candle for true love.

Contradictory? Well, not really. What this tells me is that there really is a need for this book. Most *believe* in true love. It's how to find it that's the issue.

For those of you who may be thinking; this is all very well, but my feet are already firmly in the camp of believing that I *will* find my perfect partner. Then well done. You are already half way there.

However, you may be thinking that the process is just taking far too long. When is it actually going to happen? Surely you've waited long enough, right?

## Release The Handbrake

If something you seek appears slow in coming to you, it's for one reason and one reason only. Even though you may believe in its truth, the likelihood is that you're spending more time and energy focussed on its absence, than you are on its presence. It's like driving a car with the handbrake inadvertently still on. You're only holding yourself and/or the process back.

Complaining only serves to continually feed the vibration of what it is that you *don't* want. By shifting your attention away from what is absent and focussing on what you desire its presence to be, you are reinforcing your belief in the outcome. So continue to maintain your effort, emphasis and attention towards what it is that you *do* want and its presence. And don't allow yourself any thoughts or doubts to the contrary.

In other words, forget what is and imagine the way you want it to be. Your vibration is then matched with that of your desired outcome.

Evidence of this at work can be found in more research statistics; 80% said they found their perfect partner when they least expected it. In other words, they were not focussed on why it *wasn't* happening. Its absence. Rather, because they believed it *would* happen, their energy was focussed on its presence. Then one day, lo and behold, it happened.

## I Knew It!

Let's look at this in another way…

Have you ever had a bad or negative experience happen and the first thought that entered your head was; "I knew that was going to happen"?

What's happening here is that you actually created the experience by first thinking about it. Then you gave more energy to it; the more you considered how much you *didn't* want it to happen. It may sound crazy, but it's true.

Never forget or underestimate the universal laws of attraction in play here. Like attracts like. Love attracts love, yes? So what does fear attract? Exactly. More fear.

So when you have a negative experience, one you had previously considered could happen, is it really any surprise that it did?

Our inner thoughts and feelings, what we give our time and energy to, eventually manifest themselves in our outer world. Please do not undervalue, underrate or misjudge the power of this in the search for your perfect partner. Or indeed, in *any* aspect of your life.

Now you understand the universal process by which thoughts evolve into reality, you can release the handbrake and start to create the world in which you choose to live. Including with whom you wish to share it with; your perfect partner.

Of course, what you think and do will always be your choice. But for now at least, just give some thought to how much your beliefs are playing a part in your approach, attitude and actions regarding anything that you do.

Your life and the partner you share it with, will always be the result of whatever it is you think and choose to believe. So direct your life in the way you want it to be; by thinking good quality thoughts that do nothing but serve your desired outcome.

Thus, you have started the process by which your perfect partner, your soulmate, can find you and you them.

Never stop believing.

# Reason One

## BELIEF
### In a nutshell:

'It is not what you want that you attract. You attract what you believe to be true.'

Neville Goddard

'I have been through some terrible things in my life, some of which actually happened.'

Mark Twain

# 4

# F.E.A.R.

## [Reason #2]

If 'belief' is what we often have in short supply, then 'fear' tends to appear in abundance.

Unfortunately, all too often I see people who, by allowing the fear of what could happen, permit nothing to happen. This is one thing that holds most people back in life in general, let alone in finding their perfect partner.

But what is there to be fearful about? Surely the topic of finding our perfect partner should be one of heartfelt joy, love and excitement?

Well, here are just a few examples of fear thinking that I've come across...

- What if they turn out to be the same as my ex?

- What if my friends or family don't like them?

- What if they do/don't want to get married?

- What if they do/don't want children?

- What if they turn out to be a weirdo?

- What if they're just after my money?

- What if they don't have any money?

- What if they find someone better?

- What if they're just wanting sex?

- What if they're no good in bed?

- What if they're unfaithful?

The 'what ifs'. Can you relate to any of these, or can you perhaps think of more that you could add to the list? Well here's your opportunity. We're now going to do a little exercise, so grab a pen or pencil.

First, circle the ones above that you can relate to, then write down a few of your own in the spaces provided below and on the next page. Do it now, it will be worthwhile and only takes a few seconds…

- 

- 

-

- 

- 

- 

Okay, thank you. How many on my list could you relate to? How many more were you able to add?

Now go back and consider what you have written. Between both lists (yours and mine), are there any common themes? For example: marriage, children, friends, family, work, money, career, sex, infidelity, etc.

If there are, congratulations! This is what you're most concerned about and potentially fearful of finding in your partner.

## Well Done!

I don't congratulate you with any flippancy or malevolence. Far from it. I say it with a high regard toward your ability to be both open and honest with the most important person of all in this process . . . *you*.

Being true with yourself is the most fundamental element in the practice of looking within, which ultimately will bring you what you desire in your outer world.

Some spend a lifetime unable to unearth the reason(s) they can't seem to find their perfect partner. Whereas you, because of your ability to be true to yourself and what you feel right now, have already cast light on the factor(s) that may be holding you back.

Now let's put this into some perspective...

Previously I stated that we need to be consciously aware of two topics. One we often have too much of (fear) and the other not enough of (belief). The reason I put these two in the same sentence is because there is a constant balancing act going on between the two. The more we believe, the less we fear and vice versa.

**The more we believe, the less we fear. And vice versa.**

If your belief has reached rock bottom, to the point where you no longer believe it's possible for you to find your perfect partner, then your fear is overwhelming. Conversely, if your belief is high, then your fear is minimal.

Now let's be clear here, I'm not talking about the need to become utterly fearless or gung-ho. But rather to recognise fear for what it is - a product of your own thoughts. Don't get me wrong, *danger* is real, whereas fear is a choice. You may think or feel that it's real, but in fact, the opposite is true.

The reality is that fear, the negative expectation you create in your mind, is likely to be the cause of what could be holding you back in *any* aspect of life; In your career, business and personal life, let alone a desire to find your soulmate.

## Your Inner Voice

Have you ever experienced a little voice in your head that says you can't do it? That you'll fail or you won't win? Or how about; who the hell are you to even *think* you could do it? Never mind that you're not even worthy or deserving of it. The best one of all (and the greatest prison that people choose to live in) is; what on earth will other people think?

You may attempt to reason with your inner voice by remaining positive. But its immediate response will be to question you as to the *'how?'*

All this negative inner chitchat succeeds in doing is to create overthinking, doubt and anxiety. In other words, because you don't have all the answers right now, you become fearful. Then you procrastinate and it becomes easier not to do the task than to even attempt it. We then retreat back into the security of what we know to be safe and do nothing. We've all been there.

Well, here's the good news… Fear is a liar! Yes, fears are simply stories we tell ourselves and are the biggest illusions that prevent us from living the life we want. Indeed, a head full of fear has no space for true self-esteem, love or fulfilment. So, if everything we want is on the other side of fear, how can we beat this?

It's actually easier than you think. All you need to do is understand what fear is, why it's there and where it comes from. Once you know that, you'll know how to not only disempower it, but to love it! Yes, you read that right. You can actually learn to love your fear. That's because fears are there to let you know when something is actually worth it. All you have to do is just work through it.

## Where, Why and What

So where does fear come from? Well, being negative or fearful stems from the subconscious mind drawing on either our own life experiences, or the uncertainty of the unknown. Why does it do this? It's actually there to act as a self-defence mechanism and its purpose is simply to protect us and keep us safe. It's like having your own built in security guard. So it's a good thing!

Now we know where fear comes from and why it's there, what exactly is it?

Well, we've all experienced the anxiety that comes with being fearful, yes? The dread or apprehension builds and no matter how much you attempt to reason or be logical, that inner voice in your head still manages to escalate the fear further. It then becomes so vivid, that your expectation of the event appears 'real' in your conscious mind. You can feel it, even taste how bad a future set of circumstances is going to be. Can you think of a time when this has happened to you?

Yet, how many times have you reflected, post-event and said to yourself. "That wasn't half as bad as I thought it was going to be." Sound familiar?

Yes, the illusion was actually worse than the event itself. The illusion was FALSE!

So the easiest way to remind yourself of what fear actually is and what it stands for, is to remember this simple but highly effective acronym...

F.E.A.R is simply a...

**F**alse

**E**xpectation

**A**ppearing

**R**eal

Now, by understanding and internalising this, each time you feel yourself becoming afraid, you'll be in a much better place to disempower that anxiety or fear in its infancy. In other words, you'll recognise it for what it *really* is; just a natural reaction to moving closer toward actuality.

Remember, fears are there to let you know that something is actually worth it. Your subconscious security guard is just doing its job and it wants to protect you along the way.

Henceforth, when you sense you're starting to get anxious or fearful, all you have to do is acknowledge that fear and be grateful even. Yes, thank your security guard! Sure, he or she may be a little over zealous at times, but wouldn't you rather that than the opposite?

## Afraid?

Okay, so we now know what fear is and how we can deal with it, but what then is being afraid?

Whilst fear is a noun, afraid is an adjective. In other words, being afraid is an aspect or feature of the emotion we know as fear. So being 'afraid' is the *feeling* of fear and can also be used to express concern or reluctance. Whereas fear cannot. For example…

- "I'm afraid if you do that, it won't work."

  or

- "I'm afraid I can't make it tonight."

However, my personal preference is to never use the word afraid in this context. Why not? Well, just think how it's impacting upon the foundations of your inner power and self-belief. What a disempowering affirmation!

Each time you use it, you are telling your inner self; "I am afraid…"
*Really?* You mean to say that you're actually feeling the emotion of fear
when you say it?

Why would you be *afraid* that if someone does something it wouldn't
work? What is there to be *afraid* of exactly? If you have prior
knowledge, then just delete the words 'I'm afraid', or replace them
with an alternative. So instead you could say…

- "If you do that, it won't work."

    or

- "I think/know if you do that, it won't work."

The same goes for; "I'm afraid I can't make it tonight." Why would
you be *afraid* that you couldn't make it? What is there to be *afraid*
of? Exactly what are you feeling that reflects the emotion of fear here?
Why not replace it with a simple alternative such as…

- "I'm sorry, but I can't make it tonight"

Although the alteration may seem quite minimal and unnecessary, it is
**very** necessary to your inner power and self-belief mechanisms.

Of course, it's all too easy to rationalise or excuse the words *'I'm afraid'*
as just a turn of phrase. But isn't that true of anything we say that
effects our subconscious beliefs? It's almost as bad as saying; "I don't
think I can do that." Then failing to be surprised when you can't!

So guess what? I have another acronym to help you deal with being
afraid. If F.E.A.R is nothing more than a False Expectation Appearing
Real. Then A.F.R.A.I.D is…

**A**nother

**F**alse

**R**eality

**A**ppearing

**I**n

**D**isguise

Please internalise A.F.R.A.I.D as well as F.E.A.R. These will stand you in good stead against your negative inner voice.

## Ultimate Positivity

Were you able to recall a time when you reflected post-event, that things weren't half as bad as you'd first imagined? I'm sure you did and in doing so, you have already proved to yourself that you can beat this f.e.a.r thing. Whatever it was, however bad or negative you first thought it could be, you handled it. The difference now is it's going to become a conscious effort, rather than a subconscious one.

Practising this process not only disempowers the negative illusions of being afraid or fearful, but also gives you ultimate positivity; a highly attractive aspect or feature of anyone's personality.

Positivity is contagious. So by utilising this confident and optimistic approach, a positive mindset, it will start to impact upon every area of your life. You will become a magnet for success in anything you choose to do and it starts right here; by recognising fear for what it really is, being grateful for it (thanking your security guard) and thus disempowering it.

The greatest barrier to success in life is the fear of failure. Thus, **F**alse **E**xpectations **A**ppearing **R**eal kill more dreams than failure ever will.

*"Fear does not prevent death, it prevents life."*

*- Naguib Mahfouz*

If overthinking feeds f.e.a.r, taking action sure as hell cures it. You now have the tools that will not only halt the overthinking, but also give you the power to take action. Remember, the worst mistake you can make is being too a.f.r.a.i.d to make one. So from now on make your choices reflect your desires, not your fears.

Decide that you want it more than you're a.f.r.a.i.d of it. Any fears that you fail to recognise, face up to or deal with, will simply manifest as your limits. It's as simple as that.

So what now? The simple truth of the matter is that the longer you wait for your future to change, the shorter it will be. Nobody can go back and start a new beginning, but anyone can start today and make a new ending.

Which ending do you choose?

It starts today.

# <u>Reason Two</u>

## F.E.A.R.
In a nutshell:

'The cave you fear to enter
holds the treasure you seek.'

Joseph Campbell

'The things you are
passionate about are
not random, they
are your calling.'

Fabienne Fredrickson

# 5

# **PURPOSE**

## [Reason #3]

Have you ever said to yourself, 'there must be more to life than this?' Or asked yourself, 'what on earth is *my* reason for being here?' If you have, you're not alone. Far from it. These questions bug most of us during our lifetime.

But, did you know the answers to those questions can actually provide us with health benefits? Research shows that people who feel they have a purpose in life, actually live longer. Studies have concluded that having a sense of purpose protects you against the harmful effects of stress. It also reduces the risk of death, by as much as 20% in people who have found their purpose, regardless of *when* they found it, as opposed to those who said they were more or less aimlessly wandering through life.

The internet is abundant with guidance and advice on how to find your purpose and your reason for being. Thousands of books have been written on the subject too. So why is it then that so many people still end up questioning their life and the very reason for their existence?

Think of it like driving a car. Each time you get into your car, you know where you're going and why you're going there. To your place of work, or the shops. On the school run or visiting friends and family. In other words, on all these short journeys that you make every day, you know exactly what the purpose is.

But on the biggest journey of all, your life, where you're going and why can sometimes seem much harder to identify. So how do you find this elusive 'purpose' thing?

Well, success leaves clues and successful people already know where they're going and why, *before* they start (as you do when you get into your car). In other words, they already have and are acting upon their well-defined purpose.

Now, you might be asking yourself, what on earth does knowing my purpose or not, have to do with finding my perfect partner? The answer? Everything! Because people are not attracted to what you do, they're attracted to *why* you do it.

Let's be clear here. I'm not saying that until you find *success* you won't find your perfect partner. Far from it. Rather, that if you know where you're going in life and why, you'll become very attractive indeed. And here's why…


# Fuel

Think back to a time when you were in the company of someone speaking so avidly about a subject, that you became totally focussed on their every word. To the point where you became unaware of your surroundings and lost track of time. Were you lost in the topic or absorbed by their presence and enthusiasm? The chances are that it was their energy, fervour and heartfelt belief that held your attention.

When this happens, the speakers' utter conviction and certainty becomes so compelling, that anyone listening can be sold on the topic in hand. They are displaying a sense of purpose and because this has resonated with you, you've become attracted to it.

Anyone living their life with purpose, is living their life in 3D. They're being fuelled by extraordinary Desire, Direction and Drive.

But where does this fuel come from? What is it that actually gives these people such energy and unshakable resolve? What makes them jump out of bed every morning with a spring in their step and keeps them going when things get tough? What is it that causes them to give 100% instead of doing just enough to get by, or just enough to get paid?

It is of course…

## Passion

Ah yes, that thing you can lose yourself in. That something you utterly love to do and, that when you're in the moment, the 'zone', time stands still and you no longer have the capacity to think of anything else. Almost a form of meditation if you will and the time you're at your most creative. It can be anything. But most of all, it's something that means everything to *you*.

Passion is most definitely not what anyone else says it should be. It matters not what your friends, family or society say that it is and it's no use trying to fake it either. Anyone with an ounce of intuition can smell the lack of authenticity a mile off. Can you think of a time when someone said they really cared, but somehow you 'knew' they didn't? True passion shines bright through authenticity and no words are needed to convince you otherwise. Passion cannot be forged.

So, in order to be truly passionate about anything, it has to matter to you at the deepest level of your human being. It's an ability we all possess.

Earlier, I asked you to think back to a time when you were in the company of someone speaking so avidly about a subject, that you became totally focussed on their every word. Likewise now, think of a time when *you* were talking unreservedly about something to your friends; something *you* really believe in that is close to *your* heart. Did you notice how they gave you their full attention?

You probably spoke without restraint and with complete confidence, charisma and self-assurance. In that moment, speaking with a sense of heartfelt purpose, you too were a compelling, magnetic and attractive personality.

We tend to judge others by external criteria such as their job, their age, their appearance, where they live or the car they drive etc. Whilst these external factors may be important (to some), it all becomes irrelevant if there is little or no internal value.

When meeting others (a potential perfect partner for instance), your uniqueness will be remembered by how your passion made them *feel*. So never be a.f.r.a.i.d to express what it is that you feel so passionately about. It's a **very** attractive feature indeed.

Whilst you've proved that you possess the ability to express passion, what *is* your 'why' - your ultimate goal or reason for being? What is it that could drive you to living your life with a sense of purpose?

Well, if passion is the fuel for your purpose, how do you find your very own gas station?

## The Passion Parable

Most people live just to pay the bills and then die. That isn't actually *living*, that's existing.

> *"Do it with passion or not at all"*
>
> *- Rosa Nouchette Carey*

If we were all to live by Rosa's quote, wouldn't everyone be passionate about everything they do, especially their career? Yet research has shown that as much as 80% of the workforce are unhappy. With some even *hating* what they do for a living.

So why do four out of every five people choose a pay cheque over their passion? Why do they allow themselves to live in a sometimes monotonous, mind numbing and meaningless mirage? Why do they remain solely for the money, to buy things they don't really need and to hang out with people they don't really like? Why do they live a life that just looks good on the outside, whilst on the inside they're pulling their hair out?

Instead, why isn't everyone doing what they love? Why aren't they doing what they are most passionate about and what feeds their soul?

Why aren't they doing what makes their heart sing, living their life with a great sense of purpose and living in 3D?

There are two reasons. The first is social conditioning. The second is that most people don't know what their passion is, or how to find it...

## Social Conditioning

Besides the obvious financial need we all have to make a living, there's a deeper social conditioning taking place that we've been exposed to. Advice that's been passed down from generation to generation. And it starts early, as soon as we go to school.

We're told that we must get good grades in order to get a good job. When we leave education behind and head into the workplace, we're told that we must get a good job or a safe job. A career or a profession with prospects and one with a good pension.

What is a 'safe' job in today's world? And why make a choice in our twenties based on the income it may give us in our sixties or seventies? Forty to fifty years, the majority of our time on Earth, doing something we probably don't want to do? Sounds constrictive, like being confined - imprisoned even.

Nevertheless, we endure our way through the mass process of standardisation and conformity that we call school. Then, as adults we work hard at our chosen job, career or profession.

However, whilst the advice from our older generations was no doubt well intended, it evolved for the age of the Industrial Revolution. Prior to the 19th Century, the public education system was non-existent.

So when mass education came into being, it naturally highlighted and prioritised the most useful subjects for the workplace at that time.

The basis for that standardised system still exists today, in what is now, the Technological Revolution. That's why both at school and at home, your creativity was stifled as you were steered away from what it was you liked to do, in favour of what was believed 'better' for you. The creative, expressive subjects such as music, drawing, art, dance and in some cases, sport, became low priority. Hence: 'You will never get a job doing that.'

> *"We don't grow into creativity, we grow out of it.*
> *Or rather, we get educated out if it."*
>
> *– Sir Ken Robinson*

Now let's be clear here. I'm not saying that our education system is no good whatsoever. Far from it. We all need and deserve a certain level of education to enable us to flourish in the big wide world. And some do indeed flourish extremely well, emerging with some wonderful qualifications.

There was a time, not that long ago, when you finally surfaced with your degree, it not only guaranteed you a job, but a good one at that. In recent times however, that has all changed.

Now, some young adults are emerging from the education process with their degrees, but are still unable to get that good job the 'system' had promised them. Instead they are returning home deep in debt and taking jobs they could have had years earlier. Society has changed. The way we educate has not.

Unfortunately, the whole process has dimmed our view of what 'The A List' actually is: Acumen, Aptitude and Astuteness. As a consequence, many bright, talented and highly gifted people don't believe they are. They've never had the opportunity to allow their creativity to flourish and potentially, be their true autonomous self.

## The Education System...

*"Everybody is a genius. But if you judge a fish by its ability to climb a tree, it will live its whole life believing that it is stupid"*

*- Albert Einstein*

So is it any wonder that so many people get frustrated, bitter and even angry about the path their life is taking? They're feeling restricted and want to break free from the shackles that living a conditional life has put upon them.

It's not just about their work life either. It's happening in relationships too. Social conditioning in this area has led to all sorts of untruths. For instance, that you *must* be in a relationship and if you're not, you're 'a bit weird' or there's something 'wrong' with you. That you need to get married before you get 'left on the shelf'. That you need to have children before a certain age etc.

Thus many get married and/or have children at a young age because they feel it's expected of them. Having not long emerged from their childhood and the standardised education process, they're now told to 'settle down.' How can anyone be expected to settle down when they haven't had the chance to express themselves yet?

If humans feel unable to express themselves, be it in their work, relationships or anything else, it leads toward one thing; struggle. Both internally and externally. Hence, those who know what on Earth they are here to do (their purpose), are less likely to engage in conflict or infidelity.

As we hurtle toward mankind's next level of development, the Consciousness Revolution, we will need to radically overhaul what we teach and how we enlighten the generations to come.

If youngsters can find and explore what it is that they love, what they're most passionate about and what feeds their soul, then they can live their life fulfilled with a sense of purpose. This won't just be good for the individual, but for the benefit of all mankind.

> *"Creativity now is as important in education as literacy,*
> *and we should treat it with the same status."*
>
> *– Sir Ken Robinson*

## What and Where Is It?

So how do we find this wonderful thing called passion then? Our very own gas station within, which fuels the drive towards our purpose?

Well, it's easier than you think. But first we must recognise that the need to 'find' your passion is actually a myth! It's not lost. It's not hidden under the carpet. You didn't leave it in the car and it's not with your house keys. It's neither misplaced, mislaid nor missing. You may not be able to see it, but that doesn't mean it's not there.

Folks, it is there. It's the fire in your belly that just needs igniting.

In order to ignite anything, first we need a spark. The spark that you need is simply the passion that you have. With the right fuel, that spark will turn into a flame, the flame develops into a fire and the fire becomes a furnace.

When will you know that you're living with a sense of purpose? When the fire inside you burns brighter than anything around you.

Okay, this is all well and good, but if you're still unsure as to what your passion is, then let's do a little exercise to see if we can unearth that spark …

First, grab that pen or pencil again and make sure you're in a relaxed, stress free environment. It's important that you're not likely to be interrupted and you're alone with your thoughts.

On the next page I will be asking you a question. All you have to do is to write down (or draw) the very first thing that enters your mind. It may be a word, phrase, sentence, paragraph or picture. Whatever it is, there is space for your answer.

## Imagine

Now I would like you to imagine a world - your world where you cannot fail. You're not a.f.r.a.i.d to fail and neither do you have any f.e.a.r of failure, because failure does not exist.

Take a moment right now and indulge yourself. Empty your mind of the everyday stuff that clutters it and temporarily silence that little voice in your head. Briefly, just in this moment, suspend all your doubts and concerns. Momentarily let go of perception and limitation. Take a moment to close your eyes and just be, in complete peace and at one with yourself. Remember, you cannot fail. Take as long as you need before you read the question overleaf...

Without hesitation, please write down (or draw) the first thing that comes into your head…

**If you knew, *really knew* you could not fail, what would be the <u>one</u> thing you would do?**

Write your answer here…

Well, what would you do and what would *your* world be like if you knew, *really knew* you could not fail? How different would your world be?

I appreciate that in the confines of this book, it may not be possible for you to unearth your spark, your passion, right here right now. But at least we can start the thought process. This is something I explore further in my seminars and workshops.

The first element of my Perfect Partner Programme™ is called The Compelling Compass Creator™. This is designed specifically to help unearth that spark we call passion. In turn, this can lead you to your purpose and of course, finding your perfect partner.

For those keen to explore this route more rapidly and to fast track the process, there's also the opportunity to take advantage of my Path to Purpose Plan™ which is a one to one coaching programme.

But for now, there's one final element of 'purpose' that we need to explore.

## Octane Rating

Much has been written and even more said about the need to remain positive in any situation that you face. But why exactly is that?

Well, without positivity you can remain uncertain and full of doubt and procrastination. However, by remaining positive in whatever the circumstances, you provide yourself with the correct mindset and bedrock of how to achieve anything in life that you desire. The founder of the Ford Motor Company epitomised this at its best when he said…

*"If you think you can or you can't, you're right"*

*– Henry Ford*

If passion is the fuel that drives us towards our purpose, then positivity is the octane rating of that fuel.

Whilst positivity is contagious, the same can also be said for negativity. However, a negative mind will never give you a positive life. In the same way that you can't hang out with negative people and expect a positive life.

For example; if you want to get divorced, then hang out with divorced people. Misery does love company. Conversely, if you want to be successful, then simply hang out with successful people. Yes, it really is that simple; work with chickens and you will flap - work with eagles and you will soar.

Just as having a purpose benefits our health, likewise remaining positive does too. Research has found that having a positive mindset can cut the risk of having a heart attack in half.

So how do you maintain a positive mindset? Here are two simple tips…

1. Focus on what you *want*, not what you *don't* want.

2. Always remind yourself that your blood type is 'Be Positive' (even if it isn't!)

A short story that embodies this ethos…

*Colin is in his mid-30s and is the local shopkeeper. He's rather small in stature and always wears khaki coloured overalls. He looks rather like the character Granville from the BBC TV comedy 'Open All Hours.'*

*Working in that shop was all Colin knew. For as long as he could remember, he had been in that shop helping both his father and grandfather before him. The business had been in the family for four generations, starting with his great grandfather over 100 years ago.*

*There was nothing Colin didn't know about the business. He knew the area, it's customers and local buying trends. When his father retired, Colin naturally took over the running of the business.*

*But Colin had a problem. So he sought advice from a wise old man who he respected and held in high regard…*

*"Dad, business has been good but now I fear its days are numbered. A large supermarket has opened up directly opposite and there's no way I can compete. Our shop will go broke and I feel I will have let my family down. What do you suggest I do?"*

*Colin's father, a portly man in his seventies with short grey hair that was white in places, sat in his favourite armchair which looked as old as he was. He thought carefully for a few moments only, but to Colin, it felt like an eternity…*

*"Colin, each day when you open up the shop, make sure that you give thanks for all the customers you **do** get and be thankful for the business and the profits that you **do** make."*

*A slightly puzzled Colin responded: "Okay I will. But why?"*

*"Because Colin, it's not happy people who are thankful, it's thankful people who are happy. One more thing, make sure you also do **exactly** the same for the supermarket across the road."*

*Now Colin was somewhat perplexed but he promised his father that he would be honourable to his guidance. He duly gave thanks for all his business and that of the supermarket, every day for the next six months.*

*But it was no use. Profits gradually deteriorated until the business was no longer sustainable and Colin closed the shop one last time. With a heavy heart, he went to give his father the bad news...*

*"Dad, despite doing everything you told me to do, every day for the last six months, unfortunately my prediction was correct. I've had to close the shop for good."*

*To Colin's surprise, his father smiled and said:*

*"Look what I've found in the local newspaper. That Supermarket is advertising for a new Area Manager. With your experience and local knowledge you'd be perfect for the position."*

*Colin duly got the job, doubled his income and generated additional income by leasing his premises to another business owner. Everybody was a winner and his family were extremely proud.*

So the question is: What would you have done? Even though the odds were stacked against you, would *you* have remained positive throughout?

Whilst the story embodies that 'every cloud has a silver lining', there is a much stronger force in play here. That is...

*"A positive attitude gives you power over circumstance,*
*instead of circumstance having power over you."*

*– Joyce Meyer*

## Not everyone likes peaches!

At the beginning of this chapter I said that people are not attracted to what you do, they're attracted to *why* you do it. If you know your why, your purpose, where you're going and why you're going there, you become very attractive indeed. Why? Because there's nothing more attractive than someone with passion, positivity and purpose. It's potent, powerful and persuasive.

Now, whilst you may be thinking that's great, please take heed; because right here is where so many people go wrong…

The goal is not to be attractive to everyone. The goal is to be attractive to those who believe in what you believe. The reason for this was hopefully the first thing you read when you opened this book…

'Your perfect partner is not an idealistic vision of flawless fantasy, but rather someone who supports you in your purpose and the fulfilment of your destiny, as you do theirs.'

In short, if you meet a potential partner and they don't resonate with what you believe in, then I'm sure you'd agree, it isn't going to go very far. They may look and sound great and indeed have many of the credentials you seek in your perfect partner. But they're not *your* perfect partner.

Think of it in terms of political beliefs; Imagine you were to give a talk designed to attract people to your Political Party. How many of your public audience are you likely to attract? All of them? I doubt it. The chances are, you will only attract one third of your audience; those who are congruent with your beliefs. Another third will disagree entirely and have totally opposing views, whilst the remaining third will be on middle ground.

In other words, you cannot please all the people all the time. So resist the need to be liked by everyone. It's impossible!

> *"You can be the ripest, juiciest peach in the world, and there's still going to be someone who hates peaches."*
>
> *– Dita Von Teese*

Also, it is pure folly to think you have a better chance of finding your perfect partner by simply fishing in a larger pond. Yes, there may be a seemingly inexhaustible supply of fish out there, but what's the point of investing your time and money on those who are just playing a game, or saying what they think you want to hear?

Stick to your guns and stay true to what you hold dear within. Restrict your time to those who are in accord with your heartfelt beliefs, passion and purpose. It *will* pay off. Big time.

So, find your gas station within that provides you with a never-ending supply of high-octane fuel and you will find your purpose. Then, potential suiters cannot help but be attracted to you because they too believe in what you believe.

Amongst them is your perfect partner.

# <u>Reason Three</u>

## PURPOSE

In a nutshell:

'Until you know what on Earth you're here to do, who on Earth you're meant to be with isn't going to show up.'

Tony Brown

'By failing to prepare,
you are preparing
to fail.'

Benjamin Franklin

# 6

# AVAILABILITY

## [Reason #4]

Wanting to be in a relationship is not the same as being available, or being fully prepared for one. The last emotions you need to feel when your perfect partner walks into your life, are panic, or the fear that some unfinished business is going to raise its ugly head and send them running…

The ex who still calls or even turns up occasionally, or a 'friend with benefits' who could easily sabotage any loyalty or trust issues with your new potential perfect partner. Problems with former partners, legal or financial issues, excessive demands of children, school or work that may become demanding of your time. In other words, make sure your house is fully in order, up to date and not too demanding of you.

Also, if you want your perfect partner to find you, then you can't be involved in a relationship with someone else who deep down, you know ultimately isn't right for you. The time spent with the wrong person is not only wasted, but isn't allowing you the space and availability to be found.

Those in this situation are externally sending out the wrong messages (vibrations), while internally they remain utterly convinced that their senses and their perfect partner radar are fully functioning. In other words, they believe they're aware and taking note of every possibility that comes their way. The reality is the opposite.

The signals they are actually giving out are that of unavailability and aloofness even. This is the last impression they want to give, but it happens at an unconscious level. This triggers the intuition of the potential mate (also at an unconscious level) into avoiding this person. They don't know how they 'know' to do this, but it just doesn't 'feel' right and the opportunity is lost.

## Busyness

It's a similar situation for those who *say* they are looking for their perfect partner, but have actually filled their lives with such busyness (or business if you prefer), that there's little, or no time and space available for any partner to enter. Let alone the perfect one!

That's not to say you should drop everything at a moment's notice the instant a potential perfect partner comes into view. But rather that you're open to being flexible at any given time, to allow space into your schedule for a relationship to evolve.

Again, similar to the person who is continuing in the wrong relationship; become aware of the energy and vibes you're sending out, if you're tied to your busyness.

It's all about balance and it may be worthwhile to introduce new activities into your schedule that not only get you away from work, but also provide another opportunity for your perfect partner to find you. Few are attracted to workaholics.

Let's be clear here. There are some who deliberately attract these issues into their lives, because it allows them to be so busy that they don't have the time to think about the things they are missing, or wanting in their life, e.g. a perfect partner. It's an easy self-sabotage trap to fall into; the people in this situation are either unconsciously unaware, or conscious of their actions, but will not admit it to themselves or anyone else.

## Loose ends

A perfect partner is not the escapism you sometimes seek from all your problems. Nor are they a cure for them. They can only be responsible for themselves and their life, just as you can only be responsible for yourself and your life. So it's not their responsibility to make you happy, it's yours.

This is all part of becoming emotionally mature. As we evolve, we become less dependent on looking for someone who may compensate for all our flaws, faults and failings. Sure, we all have them and no one leads a 'perfect' life, but your perfect partner will love you for who *you* are. Not for who you think they want you to be.

Imagine how you would feel to finally find your perfect partner, only to have the relationship crash and burn because you weren't fully prepared, ready or available. And it all came down to the messages (frequency of the vibrations) that you were sending out.

So, there are several benefits to dealing with any unfinished business and tidying up those loose ends in your life. Firstly, you will feel much better. More importantly, the unconscious message you'll be radiating is that YOU are not only in control of your life, but available too. A strong, positive vibration to exude and one that is very attractive indeed.

So instead, just make sure that you've done all you possibly can to be seen, heard and loved. And to do that, you need to be present, accessible and available.

Staying single and available can sometimes be hard, but it is crucial in allowing your perfect partner to find you. The frequency of the 'available' vibrations resonate at a much higher level than of those still stuck in relationships, or who are simply too busy for one.

It's your life so take control and act to attract. Remain single and available, rather than settled, stuck or swamped.

# Reason Four

## **AVAILABILITY**
In a nutshell:

'I've been single for a while now
and I have to say it's
going well….

Like... it's working out.

I think I'm the one.'

Emily Heller

'The Elimination Diet:
Remove anger, regret,
resentment, guilt, blame
and worry.
Then watch your health
and life improve.'

Charles F. Glassman

# 7

# REGRETFUL
# OR READY?

## [Reason #5]

Are you fully committed and actually ready to meet your perfect partner, or are you full of regret and maybe still a little raw from a previous relationship experience? When I say a previous relationship, I don't necessarily mean the last one either. Some people can be hung up over relationship issues from years ago.

Any hurt you may be harbouring doesn't necessarily have to come from a relationship experience. It could be from any walk of life, so it matters not if it's from a family, lifestyle or job issue. If it no longer serves you, then for the benefit of your own health and relationships with others, you need to let it go.

Whilst we need to forget the hurt that's been caused, we must not forget the lesson it taught us. What this means is, although the part that others have played in our journey is over, we can now move forward with a much better understanding of life and, more importantly, ourselves.

So who is causing the most pain here? Yes, it's easy to point the finger of blame elsewhere, especially if you're still raw and feeling hurt. But what about the emotions we feel concerning guilt, shame and regret? Where does the finger of blame get pointed then? That's right. We usually point it straight at ourselves.

Regret is the biggest agony of all and yet, we're the ones doing the pointing. Holding a grudge against yourself doesn't make you better it makes you bitter. And any bitterness or hostility you hold towards yourself is the worst form of self-disapproval. It's a form of dis-ease and therefore only serves to make you ill.

Of course, you can look back with the benefit of exact science: 'hindsight' and wish you'd done things differently. But why would you want to do that? Any decisions you made at the time were the best you could have possibly made - because they were made with what you *knew* at that time.

None of us know what we don't know and wisdom evolves from healed pain. So forgive yourself for not knowing what you didn't know before you learned it!

## The Comedy Comparison

Having the ability to get over the past can be compared to something that's funny. Yes, you did read that right! How is it that we can compare the painful regret of the past, with that of something that is amusing and makes us laugh?

Well, think of a time when you either saw or heard something so funny that it made you laugh, until it brought you to tears...

If you saw or heard it again, would it make you laugh as much? Probably not. The likelihood is that it would still be amusing, but you wouldn't laugh as hard as you did the first time and possibly, not enough to make you cry with laughter again.

What if you saw or heard it again and again? Would you keep laughing every time, or would its comedic value keep diminishing? In the end, if you saw or heard it enough, I dare say it would cease to be funny at all.

So, if we can't keep laughing at the same joke over and over again, then how is it that some people manage to keep crying about their past and those that hurt them, over and over again?

To allow a wound to heal, we need to stop touching it. Whilst the anguish may sometimes be necessary, until we realise that it's no longer needed, it will keep raising its sore, tender head.

Any bruises or soreness we may still be carrying will be spotted a long way off by any potential partner. And it doesn't matter how well we may think we've disguised it, or papered over the cracks, they will smell anxiety a mile off. When they do, their running shoes will be on and they'll disappear into the distance quicker than you can say Usain Bolt!

To make sure none of this applies to you, realise that what you resist persists, and what you accept you move beyond. This is the first step towards ensuring that you are absolutely ready and in the 'right place' for your perfect partner to find you. Why? Because you can't start the next chapter of your life while you keep re-reading the last one.

## Monkey Bars

So how can you identify when you've actually managed to let go of any regret, hurt or negative relationship history? Quite simply, it's when looking back at the past holds no interest for you anymore. Then you will know you've moved on.

But how do you get to that point in the first place? Well, getting over our past is like crossing the monkey bars in the playground. Remember that feeling? In other words, you have to let go at some point in order to move forward.

That's all well and good I hear you say, but how exactly do you 'let go'? Folks, letting go simply means to *forgive*. And most of all, forgive yourself. Because when we forgive we heal and when we let go, we grow.

Forgiveness is neither you excusing or approving of the crime, but rather that you're choosing to rise above it and you're no longer willing to be the victim. You're not doing it for the benefit of others; you're doing it because you deserve peace and wellbeing.

So forgive the situation and those involved in it. I'm not saying it's going to be easy, but life *will* get a whole lot easier for you when you do.

## Unpack

Having the ability to forgive will not only impact your life massively today, but it will dramatically influence your future too. Sure, forgiveness doesn't *change* your past, but it does change your future.

Why? Because the more anger, frustration or bitterness you carry from the past, the less capable you are of giving and receiving love in the present. The more you let go, the more open you become to receive.

Likewise, don't ever cling to a mistake just because you may have invested a lot of time (or money) into it. Any past luggage you're carrying *will* weigh you down, making you less available to be your true self.

Everything changes once the desire to move on exceeds the desire to hold on. So in order to lose any emotional weight, make sure you unpack.

## Decide

Whilst the ability to let go of the past is true strength, at the end of the day it is just a decision that you choose to make or not. Yes, it is that simple. You *choose* whether or not you continue to allow it to affect you.

What happens if you *don't* make peace with your past? Quite simply, it *will* keep showing up in your present. The past is just a place of reference, not a place of residence. So for your future's sake, choose where you're going to live.

By resisting or even refusing to forgive, you have the power to take away someone's happiness. That someone is you. And the more you hold on to it, the tighter it will grip you. Regret of the past is like drinking poison and expecting someone else to get ill! Sure, you can't change what has happened, but holding on to it *can* change you.

In order to have a better future, you will have to give up all hope of a better past. When you do this, it will feel like you've unlocked the prison gate and set somebody free, then you'll realise that actually, the prisoner was you. No one else holds the key to this gate, so you are free to leave at will. You don't require anyone's approval, permission or consent but your own. All you need to do is decide.

## Hang Up!

For those who may find the whole process of forgiveness a little challenging, then you have the opportunity to approach it from two slightly differing angles…

The first is that sometimes you don't have to 'let go' of what keeps dragging you down. Instead, just simply stop holding on to it!

The second alternative approach is that of acceptance. Life becomes a whole lot easier when you learn to accept the apology you never had. When you do this, the act of clemency takes place in your mind and it has nothing to do with the other person. Remember, you are doing this because it's *you* that deserves peace.

So, once you've let it go (by whichever method works for you), if the past does make a call, you can just hang up, because you know it has nothing new to say. Period.

Your vibe attracts your tribe. And as you've already seen in the preceding chapters, the frequency of vibrations you emit, dictate and attract those you receive. Life is an echo, so what you sow, you will reap. What you give out, you will get back.

For you to attract your perfect partner, you need to be giving off the right vibes in the first place. In other words, you need to be over any historic life experiences or relationship issues that could otherwise scupper the perfect one that's just around the corner.

Regret of the past and f.e.a.r of the future, will only serve to steal your present. Remember, your past is there to guide you, not define or confine you.

However, if you find that you can't forgive and forget, then please, just pick one.

*"Let go or be dragged."*

*- Japanese proverb*

## <u>Reason Five</u>

# REGRETFUL
# OR READY?

In a nutshell:

'Past is just a short word,
not a lifelong sentence.'

Tony Brown

'The standards you set for
yourself, set the standards
for how others will treat you.'

Tony Brown

# 8

# TERMS & CONDITIONS

## [Reason #6]

When did you last take the time to consider the Terms and Conditions (T&Cs) on anything you purchased, or on any agreement you entered into? Do you read the T&Cs when you download software from the Internet or when your iPhone gets an update? Or do you just tend to trust that it will be okay and hit 'Accept' rather than 'Decline'?

Likewise, have you ever felt that you've been caught out because you *didn't* read them? And just to rub it in you're told: "Sorry, but it does clearly state in our T&Cs…."

It's no different when looking for your perfect partner, only this time it's *your* T&Cs that are going to matter.

What do I mean by *your* T&Cs? Well, if I asked you to consider all the criteria, that a potential partner would need to have in order to be perfect for you, how many would you list?

We all consider ourselves to be open-minded don't we? However, when we begin to think about all the things we want our perfect partner to be, it's all too easy for a long list of stipulations to rapidly appear. Then, as we stand firmly and resolutely beside them, they become our defining (relationship) T&Cs. In doing so, we're reducing the gate to the field of opportunity to such an extent, that it's almost impossible for our soulmate radar to pick anything up (pardon the pun). Thus, we've inadvertently become closed-minded.

"Yes, but surely I should have standards?" I hear you cry. And of course you should. But here's where defining your T&Cs can help you to maintain your standards, whilst simultaneously keeping an open mind too. As a result, the gate to the field of opportunity becomes much wider and easier for you to open.

How exactly then, do we go about defining our T&Cs? Well, it's easier than you may think...

    (i)  'Terms' are your **non**-negotiable standards

    (ii)  'Conditions' are your more negotiable criteria.

Hence, you're able to maintain your standards whilst keeping an open mind. The best of both worlds.

# (i) Non-negotiables

Your standards are a shortlist of your 'non-negotiables', such as beliefs, behaviours and desires. These often subconscious factors are your soul food - your 'Terms'. These need to be harmonious and resonating at a certain standard for you to *remain* attracted to your partner. Your prospect may look great and be very attractive, but if they fail to match your standards, then I'm sorry, it may be fun for a while but it won't last. They are not *your* perfect partner material.

Yes, you may well have momentarily allowed your standards to slip by allowing yourself to engage, or even indulge in this relationship. But if you're serious about your soulmate finding you, then for all the reasons mentioned in Chapter 6, you need to move on.

In order to avoid falling into this sometimes oblivious trap, you need to bring your subconscious standards (Terms), into your conscious awareness. This is simply done by writing them down. Time to get that pen or pencil ready again...

What beliefs, behaviours and desires do you expect your perfect partner to have? Do their beliefs fall in line with yours? e.g. higher calling, mission or purpose. Issues you may consider trivial could be of crucial importance to them and vice versa of course. So, are you on common ground or opposing teams?

Below are twenty suggestions for you to consider as your potential non-negotiable standards...

- Fun
- Witty
- Classy
- Clever
- Happy
- Driven
- Honest

- Positive
- Dynamic
- Confident
- Passionate
- Perceptive
- Humorous
- Trustworthy
- Independent
- Knowledgeable
- Goals, dreams and desires align
- Marriage - wants/does not want
- Children - wants/does not want (anymore)
- Beliefs - both physical and metaphysical align

Now, in relation to *your* standards, i.e. your **non**-negotiables, please highlight just FIVE of the above you consider to be the most important to you. You may wish to add some more of your own, as this list is by no means inexhaustible, e.g. behaviours to do with religion, smoking, drinking or eating perhaps? Remember, these are *your* 'Terms' and very personal to you, so they're *not* up for debate. It's not what you think you *should* want, it's what you *do* want in your perfect partner.

So please do it now, take your time and give it your utmost consideration…

To illustrate how this works, here by way of example are my five non-negotiables that I had, when I was looking for my perfect partner:

- Happy
- Confident
- Goals, dreams and desires align
- Doesn't want (any more) children
- Beliefs - both physical and metaphysical align

Now you may be thinking that it's imperative there's some type of physical desirability here, such as 'good-looking', 'handsome' or 'sexy' for example. Well, for the purpose of this exercise, being physically attracted to a potential partner is a given. Why? Because, I doubt you're going to waste your time on someone who you do not find attractive, are you?

The fact is, because what we're attracted to is subjective, we can find almost anything on that list to be an 'attractive' feature – or not, as the case may be. So don't look solely for eye candy, look for soul food. If necessary, please now reconsider your list.

I accept that it may seem a little trite doing this exercise, as the answers may already be obvious (to you). But by implementing this process, you are bringing the principles that you hold subconsciously most dear, firmly into your conscious awareness. Also, it never hurts to remind yourself of these from time to time, especially if you get tempted, side-tracked, or have let your guard down!

You may be thinking: *"But I also want my perfect partner to be fun, witty, classy, clever and happy too! And that's just the first five on the list, let alone the remaining fifteen. Come to think of it, I wouldn't mind all of those as well!"* Well, we will come to that.

In the meantime, the five you have chosen should represent the core values that matter to you at your deepest level. In doing so, did you choose any amongst the last four choices on the list? If not, then please consider this…

The differing opinions, attitudes and feelings that cause the most distress and despair amongst couples, are about desires, beliefs, marriage and children. It's the expectation of these things that is at the root of all the heartache. In that case, why get into a relationship to start with, if you're not aligned in these areas from the outset?

How many times have you seen or heard examples of couples splitting up, because one wants to pursue their life in a particular direction, which fails to resonate or be understood by their partner? Or that one wants to have children or be married and the other does not?

This is when, what your potential partner believes in and what's important to them, becomes *so* important to you. Because beliefs lead to behaviour. Hence their beliefs need to resonate and be harmonious with your own.

Never underestimate the power in another's behaviour *failing* to resonate with your core values and, ultimately where that may lead.

## Take Heed

With regard to any items you may have considered in your non-negotiable standards, such as minimum levels of income, property or assets etc., then please tread very carefully. It may be a cliché, but money will not bring you happiness, or more importantly, fulfilment.

Your perfect partner, your soulmate, will be perfect for you because of the way they make you *feel*, not how much they earn or have.

So instead of having standards based on their levels of income and assets, it's far more relevant to have standards concerning their dreams, desires, goals, ambitions, mission or purpose etc.

- Do they have any?
- Does it bother you if they don't?
- Do they know where they're heading?
- Again, does it bother you if they don't?

Why are these questions so important? Because if it turns out they are your perfect partner, you'll be heading out on this journey TOGETHER. Hence, their answers need to resonate with you. Likewise of course, any potential partner needs to be in harmony with your path too.

Making the effort to take these small steps goes a long way to ensuring that the journey with your soulmate will be a wonderfully reciprocal one.

## The Benefits

Standing resolutely by your Terms, your non-negotiable standards, ensures you are radiating the message of who *you* are. Then, not only will you quickly recognise similar values in another, but they will in you too.

Additionally, you will know exactly when to bail out should their behaviour become unacceptable over issues you consider to be trivial. Remember, people don't change; they just reveal who they truly are. Plus, the size of a person can be determined by the size of the things that bother them. So, whilst knowing and radiating your standards may repel potential suitors, it *will* attract your perfect partner.

Remember; the goal is not to be attractive to everyone. The goal is to be attractive to those who believe in what you believe.

Does all of this actually work? You bet! Sure enough, my perfect partner is a very happy, confident person who also doesn't want any more children. We are mutually agreed on our goals, dreams and desires, whilst our beliefs (both physical and metaphysical) are completely aligned too. Wouldn't you agree that's a great platform from which to start a relationship?

In answer to the question earlier about the remaining fifteen suggestions, my soulmate also happens to be fun, sexy, witty, classy, clever, driven, honest, positive, attractive, passionate, humorous, independent, trustworthy and knowledgeable. Plus our views on marriage are in complete alignment too. Bingo!

So how can this happen? Surely it's just luck, right?

Well, as in all walks of life, be it your career, profession, sport, hobbies, pastimes or in finding your perfect partner; the harder you work at something the 'luckier' you get. The problem is most people are not prepared to really 'work' at finding a partner, let alone their soulmate. They either want, or worse still expect it to just 'happen'. But if you have the strength to look within, keep your mind open and believe, then it *will* happen for you too.

You will find that you can have anything you want, if you're willing to give up the belief that you can't have it. Furthermore, results will only show up when you do, so write them down and stick to *your* Terms. It's for others to either 'Accept' or 'Decline' them.

## (ii) Negotiables

Just as your standards are the non-negotiable 'Terms' of who your perfect partner should be, then your criteria are the negotiable factors, i.e. your 'Conditions'. These negotiable factors are the features of what your perfect partner may do, look like and have. Such as height, weight, size, age, eye colour, hair colour/length, children, job, income, property, assets etc. You get the picture.

However, this is where so many people inadvertently trip themselves up. They have come to believe, that in order for a potential partner to be perfect for them, they *must* have all, or most of this criteria. Yet all too often, these criteria are just a reflection of their own limitations and beliefs, rather than rational (non-emotional) thinking.

Remember, it's the Terms you set that are the five non-negotiable *must* haves, not your Conditions that are your *negotiable* ideals.

The danger here is if you continue looking and dating with all your stipulations as *must* haves, i.e. non-negotiables, then you could be unconsciously focussed and determined even, to find evidence of what it is that you *don't* want in a partner. And guess what, you will either find exactly what you're looking for (surprise surprise), or at the very least, *believe* that you have. The eyes see what the mind believes.

# Reflections

In order not to fall into this bottomless well of blinkered belief, we need to become aware of the reasons behind setting these obstacles in the first place. More often than not, they will be nothing more than a reflection of our own limitations, history and beliefs. These can be anything from keeping clear of a particular 'type', to never wanting to be married again.

Why did I refer to these as 'obstacles' and not 'criteria'? Because that's exactly what they can become; Psychological hurdles based on beliefs which usually come from an emotional place in the past, either in your own history, or worse still someone else's, e.g. parents, siblings, close friends etc.

Whilst another persons opinion is often disguised as 'good advice' and no doubt well intended, it's still nonetheless only a reflection of *their* own experiences. That doesn't make it right or wrong; it just is. Neither your own nor another persons experiences should allow your beliefs to be cast in stone. If they are, then your perfect partner may just pass you by and you'd never even know it.

An example of this is a belief I held myself for quite some time. When assessing what 'type' of woman I was most attracted to, I realised that all of my previous, serious relationships (including three marriages) had something in common; all the ladies were brown-eyed brunettes. Therefore, clearly I'm attracted to women with brown eyes and dark hair. Great! It was an easy start in my quest to identify some criteria of what my perfect partner would look like, or so I thought. She would undoubtedly be a brown-eyed brunette, right? Wrong. My perfect partner turned out to be blonde with hazel eyes!

The point here is that, if we continue to hold on to what we *believe* to be true, or what we think we need, then we may end up discounting the very person we're seeking. Also, it doesn't mean that you're NOT attracted to any opposites or variations of what you believe to be true. It's just that you may not know it yet.

So, make sure you don't do what I did and become inadvertently closed minded, because this is where the laws of attraction will stop working for you.

## Ideals

Okay, so how do you ensure that you don't become too narrow minded? Well, there are two things you can do right now - pen or pencil at the ready once more please...

Firstly, list the ideal criteria that you believe a person needs to have, in order to be the perfect partner for you. Below are a few suggestions to help get you started. All you need to do is complete your ideals alongside each criteria heading. There is also additional space for more headings of your own...

- Height


- Age


- Size

- Body type

- Weight

- Eye colour

- Hair colour

- Hair length

- Education level

- Children – do they have any, if so, what ages etc.

- Employed / Self-employed

- Job type

- Income level

- Property – do they rent, own and/or let

- Car – what type would they have

- Assets – savings, investments, property etc.

Headings of your own…

•

•

•

•

# Best Policy

Now find yourself a quiet space, somewhere you're unlikely to be disturbed or interrupted. Take each heading in turn and think of the reasons why you wrote each of your criteria.

In order to help you with this exercise, please keep in mind exactly what a belief is...

### A belief is an assumption based upon a previous experience that triggers an emotion.

So, if you decide that your criteria are based on rational thinking, then fine. However, if they're based on emotional triggers, then please stop and have a serious re-think.

Whilst any negative experience you may have encountered with a previous partner may still be raw, or fresh in your mind, it most likely did not occur because of their height, weight, size, age, eye or hair colour. Likewise it probably wasn't due to their children, job, income, property or assets either. More likely it had to do with how your previous partner *reacted* and dealt with the issues of the topic, rather than the topic itself.

I doubt your soulmate would deal with it in the same way. Wouldn't you agree?

So this is where you'll need to be completely truthful as there's nothing to be gained by kidding yourself here. Why wouldn't you want to be honest with yourself anyway? After all, it's the best policy *and* there's a huge prize at stake here too! So this is the time to be true, candid and authentic with no one else but yourself.

Completing this exercise will help you understand what beliefs your chosen criteria are based on. This in turn, will not only help you remain open minded to receive, it will ensure that you'll be utilising the universal laws of attraction to your complete advantage. In doing so, it's another huge step towards your perfect partner being able to find you.

## The 80/20 Rule

It's also worth bearing in mind that it's irrational to believe someone will possess *all* the ideal criteria you desire and have listed. So here's where you can use the '80/20 rule' to guide you...

What the 80/20 rule means is that 80% of the potential partners you encounter (four in every five), will have only 20% of what you desire.

However, 20% of those you meet (one in every five) will possess almost all (80%) of your ideal criteria.

Whilst at first this may seem a little disappointing, once again, it's worth bearing in mind what the goal is, during your soulmate search; The goal is not to be attractive to everyone, the goal is to be attractive to those who believe in what you believe.

I know what you're thinking. If it's the case that only one in every five has 80% of your ideal criteria, then how will you find someone with 100%?

Quite simply, you won't. Remember, expectation is at the root of all the heartache. So having mixed your ideal criteria recipe, you now need to add a dash of realism. But here's the taste twist; it won't matter...

Just imagine having found a potential partner who fits naturally with all (five) of your 'Terms' and 80% of your 'Conditions'. Will it really matter if they have different coloured hair or eyes than you first envisaged? Or that they're a bit taller, shorter, fatter or thinner than you'd predicted too? Does it matter what qualifications they achieved when they emerged from the education system all those years ago? Or is it more important what they've done and learned in life since? Will it matter about their past not being a model example, or is what they're going to be doing, where they're heading and why, more significant?

What *will* matter of course is the connection between the two of you and how this person makes you feel. But in order to get to this point in the first place and for the laws of attraction to be onside, you cannot afford to be closed-minded.

Looking for a partner to be perfect, by having them tick *all* the boxes, is not only a waste of your time and energy, but immensely frustrating too. This plays a major part in why so many people become despondent with the whole dating scene. Quite simply, they aren't looking for Mr or Mrs Right. What they are looking for is Mr or Mrs Faultless. And *they* don't exist.

The entire point of your 'Conditions' being negotiable, is that by not resisting, but instead surrendering to this process, you will have become wholly open minded. In doing so, your soulmate now has a far greater chance of finding you.

Never forget, what you see will always depend on what you're looking for. And your perfect partner would rather meet a mind open by wonder, than one closed by belief.

## Reason Six

# TERMS & CONDITIONS
### In a nutshell:

'The mind that perceives the limitation is the limitation.'

Buddha

'Some people find fault
like there's a reward for it.'

Zig Ziglar

# 9

# NEGATIVITY

## [Reason #7]

Do you know, or have you ever met someone who has a problem for every solution? You know, someone who always seems to create their own storms, then complains when it rains? Or how about those who spend so much time looking for faults, they have no time to correct their own? The pot calling the kettle black so to speak.

Have you also found that no matter how much you help them to see an alternative, more positive viewpoint, their misery just seems to compound? It's almost as if they've become so addicted to their anguish that nothing can get in the way of their fix.

Did you feel drained afterward too, almost as if your energy had been sapped from you?

I'm sure at some point along your journey, you'll have encountered this type of negativity. But have you ever been surprised, shocked even, as to whom this destructive energy came from? Perhaps it was delivered by someone you're close to, or someone you least expected it from?

Another persons questioning of your actions or decisions can easily leave you doubting and disbelieving in yourself. It doesn't matter whether it comes from someone you know well or not; even a stranger's negative comment said in passing, can have enormously corrosive power.

I experienced exactly this kind of negativity myself whilst searching for my perfect partner...

## Similarity

As set out in the previous chapter, having identified my Terms and Conditions, I set about informing the world . . . well, more like the south coast of England actually, about two things:

(a) who my perfect partner would be

and

(b) what we will have together.

One of the methods for doing this is of course via dating websites. So I duly crafted my 'profile' to include these two important details and posted it online.

Needless to say, especially for those who know me, what I came up with was an extremely bright, cheerful and positive outlook. And why wouldn't it be? After all, we are talking about the joy of searching for my ultimate and perfect partner here; my soulmate and the person I'm meant to be with.

Having duly publicised my profile, what sort of reaction do you think I received? Would you expect the responses to be light hearted and optimistic too? Or that of dire pessimism?

Well, the first messages I received were firmly in the camp of the latter. People I didn't know telling me that I was irrational, a dreamer and that it was not only unrealistic, but pure fantasy to be wanting all those things in a partner. Yes, the last thing I expected to get, but was actually receiving, was hate mail! Why? Because for whatever reason, these people clearly didn't believe that what I sought actually existed. So much so, that they felt it necessary to tell me.

It didn't end with strangers either. I had people who know me and even some I'm close to, tell me that what I sought would not be possible, or that if I hadn't found this person by now, then I never would. These conversations often ended with me receiving a sarcastic smile and a "good luck."

What was lucky for me, was that I'd experienced similar negativity in the past when changing jobs and career direction. Being told that it wouldn't work, that I'm not clever enough and that I'd fail. This unproductive familiarity was great experience to call upon. I'd refused to allow their words affect me then, so I wasn't about to let them now.

Can you think of a time when you've had this sort of thing happen to you? Did their words make you stronger or make you give in?

## The Inner Battle

Why is it that some people do this and how can you stop it from affecting you? More importantly, how can you ensure these negative vibes don't get in the way of you living your life the way you want and with whom you want, i.e. your perfect partner?

Well, firstly it's important to recognise that these folk are only attempting to bring you down to their level. It's not so much said to make you feel bad; it's more to do with making themselves feel better.

Secondly, understand that those who see the negative viewpoint are not at war with you at all, nor do they seek any kind of conflict. The battle they are fighting is with themselves. It's their beliefs they are wrestling with, not yours.

What you have done by expressing your wishes, desires or goals, is simply bring their discomfort and pain to the forefront of their mind.

All you can do now is politely leave them to it. It's not your job to make sense of their journey - it's theirs.

## Orange Juice

So how exactly, does any internal discomfort or pain come to be there in the first place?

It's all about what you allow into your being. An entire ocean cannot sink a ship, unless water first gets inside. Similarly, all the negativity in the world can't get you down unless you first allow it in. It's that simple.

However, if any negativity does get in, then at some point it must come out. When it does, it gets voiced and expressed. More often than not, this is what you're receiving when someone else's opinion is being communicated to you.

The late Dr. Wayne Dyer best portrays this in a short story...

*I was preparing to speak at an 'I Can Do It' conference and I decided to bring an orange on-stage with me as a prop for my lecture. I opened a conversation with a bright young fellow of about twelve who was sitting in the front row.*

*"If I were to squeeze this orange as hard as I could, what would come out?" I asked him.*

*He looked at me like I was a little crazy and said, "Juice, of course."*

*"Do you think apple juice could come out of it?"*

*"No!" he laughed.*

*"What about grapefruit juice?"*

*"No!"*

*"What would come out of it?"*

*"Orange juice, of course."*

*"Why? Why when you squeeze an orange does orange juice come out?"*

*He may have been getting a little exasperated with me at this point.*

*"Well, it's an orange and that's what's inside."*

*I nodded. "Let's assume that this orange isn't an orange, but it's you. And someone squeezes you, puts pressure on you, says something you don't like or offends you. And out of you comes anger, hatred, bitterness, fear. Why? The answer, as our young friend has told us, is because that's what's inside."*

*It's one of the great lessons of life...*

*When someone puts the pressure on you and out of you comes anything other than love, it's because that's what you've allowed to be inside. Once you take away all those negative things you don't want in your life and replace them with love, you'll find yourself living a highly functioning life.*

So, what comes out when life squeezes *you* hard? When someone says something you don't agree with, or something that hurts or offends you in some way?

If what comes out is resentment, jealousy, bitterness, anger, fear or any kind of negativity, it's because that's what is already inside. And it doesn't matter who does the squeezing either; your parents, siblings, children, partner, neighbour, boss, the company you work for, or even the government. If anyone says or does something that you don't like or agree with, what will come out of you is what's already inside. And what's inside is entirely up to you, because it's your choice as to what you allow in.

> *"Don't let negative and toxic people rent space in your head.*
> *Raise the rent and kick them out!"*
>
> *- Robert Tew*

## The Effects

I don't believe that anyone sets out to be negative. After all, we aren't born this way; we're born as happy, inquisitive and curious children giving love unconditionally. As Dr. Wayne Dyer explained in his story, it's what we've come to allow into our being. But what effect does it have *upon* our being?

Let's assume that there's an amazing pill you can take that can change your physiology in seven different ways. Let's say it can:

1. Increase your heart rate
2. Increase your blood pressure
3. Create excess hormones
4. Create unwanted acid
5. Decrease your aura
6. Effect your body language and
7. Decrease your power and resilience

Would you take such a pill? Probably not. Yet this is exactly what you give your consent to each time you allow negativity in.

If these are the effects it has on the recipient's body, imagine what it does to others when the misery wants to be shared or offloaded. Is it any wonder then that you feel drained and your energy has been sapped when talking to such a person?

As negative emotions are explained or get shared, power is added. That's because any energy being resisted is actually being fed. Anything being pushed away is being invited to stay. Therefore, what you resist persists.

So how do we reverse this process and release any negative attraction? Simply by taking our attention away from it by focusing on what we want, not what we don't want. Sound familiar?

## The Safeguards

It doesn't matter how much of a positive person you believe you are, the reality is, that at some point, we *all* have negative thoughts of one kind or another. So how do you keep these thoughts from becoming all consuming and ensure that you don't become hooked on the negativity too?

Well, to ensure that you too don't free-fall into this caustic chasm, all you need is the ability to recognise what is happening, when it's happening and then to act immediately when it does...

Firstly, stop and consider whether your thoughts (or the thoughts of others) serve your wishes, desires and goals. If they don't, destroy the negative thoughts when they first appear, because this is when they're at their weakest. In other words, you don't allow them to take root and grow; you nip the negativity in the bud. The pessimistic addict is consumed purely because they've allowed their saplings of negativity to grow to such a point, they can no longer 'see the wood for the trees'.

Next, stay away from 'still' people - those who are still unhappy, still complaining and still getting nowhere. Also protect yourself from those who always seem to be full of self-pity and consider themselves 'victims'. You know, the ones who are full of woe all the time.

If for any reason you find that you're unable to shield yourself from these folk (family, work colleagues etc.), then at least recognise what they're repeatedly putting themselves through and promise to never inflict such self-harm on yourself. Why does misery love company so much? Because it somehow feels 'safer' to be in the same boat as everybody else, doesn't it?

So what happens if you do momentarily let your guard down and find such people planting their seeds of doubt and despair in your garden? All you have to do is simply act immediately. Take responsibility for your own thoughts and feelings and tell yourself to stop being a victim too.

The worst thing you can do is nothing at all. *Inaction* only serves to feed fear but *taking action* banishes it. When you do, you'll be amazed at just how quickly any doom and gloom can be forgotten. In doing so, you'll have nipped the negativity right where it's needed; in the bud . . . before it takes root.

The bottom line here is, if you don't wish to be exuding the negative vibrations that drain those around you, including that of any potential partner, you need to jump ship from the vessel of victims and swim as fast as you can to the land of positivity and solutions. When you do, you'll be surprised just how close it actually is. All you require is the resolution to seek it.

What do all these metaphors mean? It means that you don't have to make a hard journey more difficult. Yes, sometimes you may have been given a cactus to travel with, but that doesn't mean you have to sit on it! If you prefer, without the metaphor then yes, you may have had a bad day, but was it a bad day, or was it just a bad five minutes that you milked all day?

## Declarations

Getting back to my online dating profile, I can happily report that I also received two other types of response; those that were positive about the things that I'd said and those who appeared indifferent to them.

Of the three types received, which do you think I chose to respond to? Those that were...

- (a) negative
- (b) neutral
- (c) positive?

Yes, only the positive ones of course. Consequently, my example confirms both declarations that we've already discussed in this book. That is:

- The goal of only being attractive to those who believe in what you believe and
- Resonating with one third of your audience.

Needless to say, I duly met some wonderfully likeminded and positive people, including of course, my perfect partner! ☺

My example doesn't mean that you too need to utilise the medium of online dating, but rather be aware and never lose sight of these two declarations.

# Façade

Your perfect partner won't be able to find you and probably won't want to either, if you're camouflaged in a shroud of negativity. If you've never enjoyed listening to someone whine, whinge or complain, the chances are that no one enjoys listening to you do it either.

So please keep in mind that the relationship you have with yourself, sets the tone for every relationship you will have. Take the time to remove any potential cloak of negativity that may be disguising the real you and replace it with one of love and kindness. After all, you do have a lot of this to give don't you?

In doing so, every time you remove harmful negativity from your life, you're creating more space for love and positivity.

Remember, be careful what you choose to allow in. What's inside *will* manifest outside.

# Reason Seven

## **NEGATIVITY**
In a nutshell:

'Your worst enemy cannot harm you
as much as your own unguarded
thoughts.'

Buddha

'Love didn't hurt you.
Someone who doesn't know
how to love hurt you, and
you confused the two.'

Tony Gaskins Jr.

# 10

# EXILED OR EXCITED?

## [Reason #8]

Picture the scene; an enormous castle surrounded by a deep, wide, crocodile infested moat. The only means of access into the fortress is across the massive drawbridge, which spans the dangerous waters.

Even if the drawbridge has been lowered, there is still the tall and very heavy iron gate to raise, before reaching the locked castle door . . . a fairly impenetrable and easy to defend place of refuge.

I'm sure that many of us, at some point, have retreated and withdrawn into our own emotional castle - a fortress of self-induced exile. A place of sanctuary where we feel safe and from where we vow to never be hurt again. Have you ever heard someone referred to as still having their walls or defences up? This is often where they've gone.

# Wounded

After a negative, emotional experience, many not only retreat behind their walls, but also lock the castle door, drop the iron gate, raise the drawbridge and starve the crocs. Thereby ensuring that their heart cannot be found and should anyone be foolish enough to make the attempt, they'll get eaten alive!

Understandably their heart and more importantly, their real self, cannot be found for the overwhelming fear of being hurt again. I'm not saying it's wrong to do this, especially for a short period of necessary grieving, thinking and regrouping, but rather to be consciously aware of what can happen next...

Rather than appearing from the emotional castle more worldly wise, open minded and receptive, the fear of experiencing the same hurt again is so real, that some remain in exile for years. The danger here is that whilst they've been licking their wounds, all their energy has been focused on the aspects in a partner that they *don't* want.

# No Apology

Whilst we've already discussed the topic and the impact of focussed negativity within these pages, I make no apology for covering it once more. For I have found that this is the biggest barrier to people achieving their heart's desire. And, not just with regard to finding their true love and perfect partner either, but in every aspect of life. I cannot stress the importance of this subject enough.

Those who place themselves in exile for too long may become so engrossed in their emotional pain, that they unwittingly become focussed on the negatives (what they don't want) rather than the positives (what they do want). The result is that they simply end up attracting into their life exactly what they *don't* want!

Have you ever heard, or know of someone who always seems to attract the wrong type of partner into their life? This is why. They are focussed on what they wish to avoid, rather than what they wish to have. As we already know, underestimating the universal laws of attraction is pure folly. Like attracts like and love attracts love. So what does fear attract? You already know the answer to that one.

Herein lies the danger; that which we think most about is what we create. We construct it by first thinking about it and then we give it more energy, power and momentum by focussing our attention on it. Hence we make it happen. Hardly surprising then, that when we look for fault, sure enough, that's exactly what we find.

The eyes see what the mind already believes.

## Reasons

Another aspect to consider when getting through a traumatic experience is that quite simply, everything happens for a reason. Can you think of a time when something awful happened, only for you to see the bigger picture and understand the reason for its occurrence at a later date?

Granted, having the ability to understand the reason whilst in the despair of the moment is nigh on impossible. But even when at this point, just *knowing* and *accepting* that there is a greater reason, is not only comforting, but can also aid the speed of recovery too.

When we find ourselves at such a crossroads, "Why?" is the question we struggle to find the answer to. It's because we're so close to the issue that we cannot see the bigger picture. So what can we do to help ourselves and find the apparently unfathomable solution?

In order to see the wider view, it sounds obvious, but we just need to take a step back, sometimes several strides. I know this is easier said than done, but think of it this way; have you ever stood and admired a picture or painting on a wall? Did you stand right up close to it, or did you take a few steps back to take it all in and benefit from its full impact?

Likewise, when driving your car, have you ever been too close behind a large truck, so close that it felt uncomfortable and you couldn't see anything else? Or perhaps you wanted to overtake the truck, but again couldn't see anything of the road ahead? What did you do?

It's the same in life. If you want to see the bigger picture, you need to first pull back before you can move forward. Just like driving your car and overtaking the truck, this process can take a little practise. Again, just *knowing* and *accepting* that indeed, there is a bigger reason other than the hurt you're experiencing in that moment, will assist you no end in moving forward.

Understanding this process helped me immensely, after I experienced a painful and rather puzzling break-up. When we met, she was divorced and had been estranged from her children for some years. We made a happy couple. She moved in and we made a happy home together. Then amazingly, her children came to spend more and more time with us. It was delightful to see and became clear that they wanted to be living with their mother again. So we duly started to make plans for a future together, for all of us. But before I knew it, she was gone.

An opportunity had arisen to take a property close to both her work and the children's school. Yes, it was ideal, but where did I fit in? Quite simply, I didn't.

Whilst extremely puzzling at the time, the bigger picture was that our relationship had brought her together with her children and they became reunited as a family once again. How wonderful is that? She is now happily married too.

There is always something greater than ourselves going on. We just need the eyes and mind to see it. So how can this craft be practised? By simply looking back on some key moments in your life and considering the impact the event had upon others. If you hadn't had the traumatic break-up with 'X', then you would never have met 'Y' and so on.

So train your mind to see the good in every situation. I'm sure you'll be able to witness some amazing views as you look back.

## Keys To Fit Your Locks

Instead of manifesting the traits we *don't* want in any partner, how do we turn it around and have any chance of attracting what it is we *do* want into our lives?

Well, as our inner thoughts eventually manifest themselves in our outer world, imagine what life could be like if we made all the things we think about, focus on and give our attention to, positive thoughts about what it is we *do* want. Wow! That sounds great, but how do we actually go about manifesting this shift in our thinking?

As we already know, all we have to do first is acknowledge why the fear is there in the first place; it's there to protect us. So, remember to thank your sometimes overzealous security guard. Next, remind yourself of what f.e.a.r is and what it stands for (Chapter 4).

By becoming consciously aware of your thoughts and doing these two simple things, firstly acknowledging your f.e.a.r and secondly recognising it for what it really is, you will in fact disempower it. It really is that easy. You can then become focused upon and will attract, all the things that you *do* want into your life.

By doing so means that your perfect partner now has a much better chance of finding you. Whilst your soulmate possesses the key to your castle door, you still need to have appeared from exile, by raising the gate, lowering the drawbridge and of course, making sure those crocs have all been fed.


## It's What You're Made Of

It's all to do with emotional openness. That is, to first be aware, then to express and finally to have the desire to share ones heartfelt emotions.

In other words, don't save your love up for a rainy day, instead give it away and show people it's what you're made of. Does that mean being vulnerable? Maybe. But in order for love to find you, first you must allow it the space to attract and manifest.

Love comes to those who still believe after betrayal and who remain expectant after exclusion. The love of your life can appear after the mistake of your life. So if you can love the wrong person, just imagine how much you can love the right one.

Your perfect partner doesn't want to meet someone who is resigned to self-induced exile and emotionally unavailable. They want someone who's not a.f.r.a.i.d to show their love. This is an incredibly powerful frequency to emit, as people always desire to listen to love rather than fear.

Likewise, soulmates recognise each other by loving vibes, not by how much people blame and complain. Let's face it, who would you rather meet?

The laws of attraction are universal and you *will* get what you think most about. So always think positive thoughts and remain focused on what it is you *do* want, not what you don't.

The joy and pleasure to be found in searching for your soulmate isn't daunting, it's exciting!

So please, if you haven't done so already…

Leave the castle.

# <u>Reason Eight</u>

## **EXILED OR EXCITED?**
In a nutshell:

'No matter what commandments, sutras and religious or spiritual stuff you follow, if you choose love, you win. That's it.'

Tanya Markul

"The quieter you become,
the more you can hear."

Ram Dass

# 11

# RECOGNISE & RESPOND

## [Reason #9]

Do you know that not all questions can be answered by Google? This may seem a daft question, but the only skill required to find answers today, is to simply type the question on a keyboard and the answers to anything and everything are at the tips of our fingers. Well, almost everything; the answer to "How do I find my soulmate?" isn't *so* easy to find.

Ironically, when it comes to matters of the heart, it *is* your heart that has the answers. The only skill required now is to silence your head long enough for you to actually hear them.

This is especially true when it comes to recognising and responding to opportune moments, when they occur in our everyday lives. Yes, you know you *could* do that (heart), but can you be bothered? (head). And do you *really* want to go to all that effort? (head again). The mind often comes up with lots more negatives that easily outweigh the positives.

So how can we revert the balance in favour of the optimistic potential? Well, in order to get our minds to be more accepting, we just need to acknowledge two things - intuition and trust.

For the moment, let's assume we've now managed to get our minds to this place of compliance and that we've successfully tipped the balance in favour of the positives. Excellent! Now what?

Nothing will occur without the ability, courage and strength to take action. In other words, just knowing and acknowledging your intuition and trusting the process is worthless, unless it's acted upon. I meet far too many people who, whilst they do truly believe that their soulmate exists and that the universe will provide and manifest them, actually do little or nothing to make it happen. They're just sitting around waiting. And, because it hasn't happened yet, complaining too.

In this chapter we will not only look at recognising our intuition and our trust in the process, but also how we need to respond, in order to manifest that which we seek.

## Intuition

Sometimes our best decisions aren't made with our minds; they're made with our instinct. Somehow we just 'know', without knowing *how* we know.

Often referred to as our unconscious knowing or 'gut' instinct, intuition is a sense; a feeling we recognise and acknowledge that we just 'know' to do something. So much so, it feels right even before we do it! This is our unconscious mind, our intuition, our heart and the universe even, directing and guiding us towards that which we seek.

Can you think of a time when your intuition told you to do something and it turned out to be completely correct? On that occasion you (hopefully) took notice. Excellent. But how often do we belittle or plainly ignore the little serendipitous moments and messages we're being given? And not just in relation to finding our soulmate either. How often do we miss opportune moments in any aspect of our lives? Regrettably, it's too often.

More frustrating is that it's almost impossible to gauge or measure. How would you know your soulmate was at that party last night? You know, the party you cried off from at the last moment because you couldn't be bothered to go. Or that they were in the café you passed by when you had a really strong desire for coffee, but chose to ignore it.

Life is not 'happening' to us, life is 'replying' to us. In other words, life is 10% what happens and 90% how we respond to it . . . or not.

Sometimes it feels like it's just chance, when actually we're being guided to that which we seek. At the end of the day, what's the risk? Isn't the potential outcome far worthier of the effort required to just act upon it?

Sometimes we have to stop thinking so much and just go where our heart, intuition and gut guides us. In other words, to just go with the flow. In doing so, we don't become overly concerned with the details, the 'how to's' or the 'what ifs'. Overthinking is the art of creating problems or issues that never existed. At best it creates procrastination, at worst inaction.

Next time, make sure you go to that party and stop and have that coffee. What's the worst that can happen? Sure, there's no guarantee that you'll meet your soulmate at either venue, but maybe you'll meet them as a *result* of being there, e.g. on the way home, or bumping into a friend who's been meaning to introduce you to someone.

If it still feels like you're taking a chance, what the hell - take it anyway! The cost of *not* taking a chance and following your heart is spending the rest of your life wishing you had.

The inspiration you seek is already within you. You just need to *trust* it.

# Trust

In order for our perfect partner to find us at all, we must raise our frequency and vibration, as I often refer to in this book. 'Trust' is another way of doing this. But what exactly is it?

Trust is the ability to place our confidence in someone or something else. This often means in something we cannot see . . . our intuition for example.

The problem some people have with trust is that they're too fearful of making a decision, in case it turns out to be the wrong one. Why do we do this? Social conditioning.

We're taught from a young age that we must know the right answers. This is reinforced by constant testing and exams from as early as five years old. The result of this schooling process is that we become too afraid to make a decision - in case we're wrong. Many people have become *so* fearful of being wrong, that they've actually become addicted to the need to always be right. Perhaps you know such a person? If you do, please remember that it's not their fault…

As children we're naturally happy, curious and trusting. We're pretty fearless too and certainly not afraid of being 'wrong' either. Until that is, we're guided towards having to know the answers, then tested and graded on them according to our 'intelligence'. Consequently, our learning to trust and to not be afraid of being wrong gets gradually taught out of us. This affects some more than others.

Naturally, this approach and attitude then gets carried into adulthood and into the jobs, offices and companies we work at. Not only that, but into our everyday personal lives too. In other words, we end up wanting to 'see' the answers or the results of what our decisions will bring, *before* we make them (in case we're wrong). In these situations, both our intuition and creativity becomes stifled.

But here's the thing; you don't need to see what's at the top of the staircase before you take the first step. You just need the courage (trust) to take that step in the first place.

It's a fact that the only impossible journey is the one you never embark upon. Maybe it won't work out, but seeing if it does or not, could actually turn out to be the best journey ever. Sometimes, the smallest step can end up being the biggest step of your life. Tip toe if you must, but take that step.

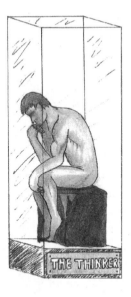
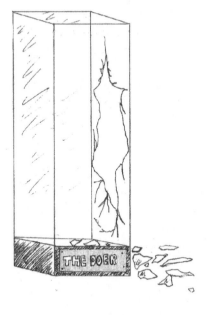

Also, be mindful that there's no such thing as failure, only results. In other words, either you'll win or you'll learn. Sometimes, not getting what you want can be a marvellous stroke of luck e.g. that job you failed to get, only to be offered a better position elsewhere. That move to a new house, which fell through, only for you to find a better property a week later. I'm sure you can think of many similar examples that have happened to you.

So, in order to find what you're looking for, all you have to do first is recognise how these serendipitous moments are guiding you, then respond positively by acting upon them.

Having trust alone in the process will *not* be sufficient. You must act upon your instincts. In doing so, you are reaffirming to the universe that which you desire. In other words, you first need to sow in order to later reap.

Also, never allow another's opinion of what's right or wrong to affect you; confidence is silent, it's the insecurities that are loud. Besides, the one who trusts their path has no need to prove another is wrong, because there is no right or wrong, there just is.

Finally, never let go of your vision and trust in the 'I AM' process; Intuition, Attraction and Manifestation.

Life begins at the end of your comfort zone and you *will* miss 100% of the shots you don't take. This is your game of life, so just play it, live it and take the shot. If you miss, take it again… and again. Repeat as necessary.

We all make choices, but in the end, it's our choices that make us. So trust yourself; for you know more than you think you do.

# Intent

Does trusting your intuition have any *real* impact on your life? The answer to this question lies in how you choose to *live* your life, i.e. do you live more out of habit than intent?

Those who choose to live more or less within the same habitual pattern, will sure enough find life repeating itself and little or nothing will change. I'm not saying that this is either right or wrong, it just is. And it may just be what someone desires, which is okay for them, if they don't want anything to be different in their life. Some may do this to avoid any form of criticism (social conditioning again). Yet the only way to be completely proficient at avoiding any form of disapproval is to say nothing, do nothing and *be* nothing.

If you desire more and want to become more, then you must choose to live less out of habit and more out of intent. Then and only then, can you make things happen. This is because nothing whatsoever happens without intent. Not one single thing has ever been accomplished without it. So your intention is everything. It is creation.

By living out of intent and trusting your intuition today, you will indeed begin to form the future in which you wish to live. And what's the best way to predict the future? Create it.

I'm not saying it will be all plain sailing, but rather the distance between your dreams and reality is called intent and action. So don't ever be upset with the results you didn't get from the action you didn't take. Live out of intent; trust your intuition and act by recognising and responding to it.

Little by little will soon become more and more as you start to see the results manifesting in your life. Vision without execution is called hallucination and the longer you wait for your future to change, the shorter it will be.

The fact that you're reading this, tells me you're someone who desires more for yourself. Not only that, but you've already displayed both intent *and* trust in your intuition. There's a reason this book is in your hands - you intended it. Your intuition suggested you pick it up, or a friend did by recommending it to you (because of your intent). Either way, you trusted it. So you've already proved that you can do this.

To now get the specific results you desire for yourself, e.g. finding your perfect partner, all you need do is be truthful with the most important person in this process... YOU.

Eleanor Roosevelt once said, 'The future belongs to those who believe in their dreams'. I would add to that by saying they should also trust their intuition and have the strength to take action. Do not be afraid to walk your talk, be the type of person you want to meet and above all, be consistent.

Your intent is your creation. Trust the process, recognise and respond to your intuition and the results will sort themselves out. In other words, by acting positively towards those serendipitous thoughts and moments, you will be positioning yourself for your perfect partner to find you.

Finally, follow your instincts and not the crowd. If it helps, the next time you consider following the masses, just remember that the 'm' is often silent.

You are in tuition.

Trust it.

# <u>Reason Nine</u>

# **RECOGNISE & RESPOND**
### In a nutshell:

## 'Opportunities multiply as they are seized.'

Sun Tzu

'Cinderella never asked for a Prince. She asked for a night off and a dress.'

Kiera Cass

# 12

# **RELAX**

## [Reason #10]

Relax at the thought of ever meeting your soulmate. Yes, that's right, just chill.

Having done so much to attract and manifest this person into your life, relaxing at the thought of ever meeting them may now seem a little bizarre. However, doing so *is* completely necessary, as it's the last part of the process, prior to actually meeting your perfect partner.

It's vital that you are now calm, collected and composed. Why? Because you need to be in a place where you're not only totally at ease with the work you've done, but also content with who *you* are.

## **Acceptance**

If one of the hardest things in life is finding out who you *really* are, then most certainly the next is accepting what you find. And for your soulmate to be able to find that person too, then you already need to be there.

Think of it this way; how can you expect your perfect partner to accept you for who you are, if *you* haven't done so? Likewise, how can you expect them to love you, if you don't already love yourself?

In order to love yourself, you need to accept yourself. To be able to accept yourself, you simply need to let go and stop holding on to the past. Remember, regret of the past and fear of the future only serves to steal your present. In this case, it's robbing you of the chance to find your soulmate.

I often hear people refer to finding their soulmate as the need to find the last piece of the puzzle, thinking that when they do, their lives will be complete. But the reality is there are no pieces missing, because *you are* the puzzle. You are whole and all the pieces are already there. All that's required is to go through the process of fitting them together. When you do, you'll see the bigger picture of who you truly are.

It's when people are not able to do this, or they don't want to, that they feel there is something missing. Then they conclude that the 'something' missing is a partner and by finding one, it will complete them. Herein lies the miscalculation of innocent expectation that only leads to the rollercoaster ride of rocky relationships.

Some, having experienced this relationship rollercoaster, decide to exit and go their own way. But because they don't change their mindset - i.e. they don't first look within; they end up back in the queue for a different seat on the same scary ride.

So what mindset adjustment can you make that ensures you don't end up standing in the same queue? The answer is so simple, yet so powerful and it's all to do with acceptance...

**Accept that you don't need someone to complete you. You only need someone to accept you completely.**

Of course it's entirely possible that someone could accept you without you having already done so. However, such an ill-balanced scenario can only lead to an ill-fated relationship. This is because the acceptance is not 'complete'. Its completeness comes when *both* parties fully recognise, acknowledge and accept who you really are. Soulmates of course, will be equally accepting of each other.

Think of it this way: If I asked you to list all the things you love the most, how long would it take you to put yourself on that list?

As we now know, love of oneself begins with acceptance of oneself. Therefore, for someone to accept and love you completely, you need to have done so first.

## Your 'Team'

Having done the work necessary to attract your perfect partner, you can now relax at the thought of ever meeting them. I'm not suggesting that you no longer need to continue with the self-development, awareness or visualization exercises, as personal growth is always a 'work in progress' assignment. However, you do need to let go of the consequence.

In doing so you will put your trust in other energies and forces to act on your behalf. This is your 'team' of instincts if you will. Your heartfelt thoughts, subconscious and love, all emitting a frequency of vibration that will utilise the universal laws of attraction to your complete advantage and work in harmony to bring about all you desire.

Furthermore, believing and trusting that you will indeed meet your soulmate, puts you in an entirely different place. A place of knowing that something *will* happen is not only a relief, but also a release of any self-proclaimed pressure. This enables you to go about your day without any self-doubt or repetitive thoughts of whether or not it's ever going to happen. Instead, thoughts of the unknown become 'when' not 'if'.

So do not hide from love. Do not store it up and do not go looking for it. Instead, love unconditionally and live your life by giving love away. Then wait for it to come back tenfold. This is where patience comes into play…

## Patience

Patience is the calm acceptance that things can happen in a different order to the one you had planned or imagined. Patience is therefore proactive and a form of action (the practise of power even).

Patience is not the ability to wait, but your attitude *whilst* you are waiting. It is a key element of success as it reflects your acceptance, belief and trust in the process of attainment.

Once you've decided that it's time to find your perfect partner, how long will it take? Well, as much as we all desire some kind of inevitability, of course, nothing is certain. But one thing *is* for sure; it's not like flicking a switch, so they probably won't turn up on your doorstep the very next day!

What *will* determine the amount of time it takes will be attributable to your own personal beliefs, attitude and the extent of action you decide to take (or not). In other words, the results you manifest and the time it takes to do so, will differ immensely between you paying 'lip service' to it, or pouring your heart, soul and complete being into it. For example...

## Destiny?

From the time I started dating in my mid-teens, finding my perfect partner took some forty years. Granted, most of this time was not spent consciously aware of the power of intent. It was more spent unconsciously unaware and allowing life to just 'happen'.

Don't get me wrong, life had been great and I'd achieved as much success in business as I had in motor racing. But after three divorces, the same could hardly be said for my love life.

After that conversation with Wendy, I decided to pour my heart, soul and complete being into finding the person I'm here to be with. The alternative to that for me was to remain single, as I decided I'd rather be on my own than be in the wrong relationship.

That level of heartfelt commitment, desire and yes, vulnerability too, brought about a transformational period of personal growth that otherwise may never have happened. From the self-realisation of all I have imparted in this book, finding my perfect partner didn't take very long at all - less than two short years in fact.

Was it destined that our paths would someday cross anyway? Well, it transpired that we had already come close on several occasions...

Thirty-six years previously, when we were teenagers, our parent's houses were just three miles apart. Seventeen years later and more than 150 miles from where our parents lived, we had both independently moved to the same town. This time we were just 100 metres away from each another.

We both then remained in the area for almost twenty years before we finally met. Unbeknown to either of us, during this time, we had several mutual friends too. Had our friends introduced us earlier, would it have worked out? Absolutely not. The timing would never have been right. At any given time previously, each of us were either unavailable (in another relationship), or not in the right place.

So was it just coincidence that we did finally meet? I think you already know my thoughts on that one.

The principal here is not one of patience, destiny or fate, but rather of self-actualisation, intent and timing. In other words, you simply need to be in the right place, at the right time. This doesn't mean going to every party and stopping at every café. Being in the right 'place' has nothing to do with the venue. It has everything to do with *you*.

# Ripples

What about that 'timing' thing? Well, whilst timing may be everything, there is only one issue about time that matters with this topic. And that is the amount of time you put into becoming the person you wish to meet. It can and will happen, but only once you're in a place of knowing, accepting and loving who you really are first.

Does that mean being open, honest and willing to be vulnerable too? Well, it certainly does if those are the qualities you seek in your partner. In order for you to attract the partner you want, you need to display and exude the exact same qualities you desire in them.

By now, I'm sure you realise that this is nothing more than vibration; frequency and resonance at work again. Like attracts like etc. To create ripples in a pond, someone has to drop the first pebble. That person is you.

Is it hard to do? Not really. You just have to *want* to do it. Those who don't wish to, for whatever reason, will simply find an excuse. In my experience most people want the rapid answer, the quick fix or to just be given the 'secret', so they can get on with whatever is the next, most urgent thing in their lives. This is the repetitive trap that's so easy to fall into. Just as the habitual dieter doesn't do it right in the first place, they always end up looking for the next best thing, advice or tip that's around.

The moral here is just the same; if you're looking for long-term results, don't seek a short-term fix.

Whatever *you* do, don't put yourself under any pressure. Any negativity, burden or stress you carry towards your goal, will influence the outcome with negative effect.

So take your time. Work on your self-realisation, set out your intent, live by it and relax. Accept, believe and trust in the magnificence of the process and allow your team to do their work.

Most of all, enjoy the journey.

It's all great fun.

# <u>Reason Ten</u>

## **RELAX**
In a nutshell:

'Two things define you:
Your patience when you have
nothing and your attitude when
you have everything.'

Imam Ali

'Formal education
will make you a living.
Self-education will make
you a fortune.'

Jim Rohn

# 13

# AROUND THE CLOCK SUCCESS

This book has been written as a guide to help you position yourself so that your perfect partner, your soulmate, can find you. The ten areas covered are by no means exhaustive, but they are the most common reasons as to why your soulmate has yet to track you down.

Of course there are exceptions to every rule and I have no doubt that you may even know someone who has succeeded, where others have failed. The blissfully happy couple who met whilst one (or both) of them were already in another relationship. The friend with the perfect partner who had helped overcome the trauma of a previous relationship. Yes it *can* happen. When it does, it is the exception rather than the rule.

So, instead of being one of the majority out there just hoping to be found, following this book and implementing its intentions will position you as one of the few who are actually poised, in the right place and *ready* to be found.

## Imaginary Friend

Your journey towards finding your soulmate may well be one of self-awareness, discovery and development and that's fine. In fact it's ideal. The most important part of this process is to simply be you. In other words, don't be the person you think others want you to be, what you believe society expects you to be, or worse still, what you think your perfect partner would want you to be.

I come across this a lot; people attempting to reflect what they *think* a partner ideally desires in a friend, companion and lover. And this simply doesn't work. It may do in the short term, but never in the long run.

Firstly, it's only what you *think* they want. Secondly and perhaps more importantly, do they actually *know* what they want yet? So please, save yourself any unnecessary overthinking and don't strain to be somebody you're not.

> *'Be yourself; everyone else is already taken.'*
> *– Oscar Wilde*

Likewise, don't attempt to change someone to effect the appearance of who you'd like your soulmate to be. And never change someone to make you happy either – unless of course, that someone is *you*.

## The D Principle

Attracting our perfect partner is all to do with what we emit, not what we omit. In other words, it's about what we radiate and exude of our true selves, rather than what we think may be lacking or missing.

Everything we do, every action and every thought is energy. And just like dropping that pebble into the pond, there is a ripple effect, a resonance and a consequence to those thoughts and actions. It's the frequency of this resonance that attracts the consequence of what we think and do.

Have you ever heard of someone being on the same 'wavelength', or couples 'in tune' with one another? This is because their thoughts and actions are resonating at the same frequency. This is where attraction occurs.

What happens to couples that once resonated so well together, who were once on the same wavelength, in tune and clearly on the same frequency – why do they split up? How is it that over time, they can go from being immensely attracted to one another, to the point of repelling and rejecting each other?

It all comes down to The D Principle:-

- Difference
- Discord
- Disagreement
- Dissention and
- Disharmony

All of which equals Dissonance, and if they're married, Divorce too.

Dissonance is simply the opposite of resonance. What this means is that the couple that were once so close, are no longer resonating on the same frequency. This happens as the pressures of everyday life start to push and pull us in different directions and our vibrations begin to change frequency.

Have you ever heard someone say that their partner doesn't understand them anymore? Or that they're growing apart or feel they're being left behind? Maybe you've had some or all of those thoughts yourself at some point? This is the evidence of dissonance. Where one's frequency is starting to differ from the other.

For whatever the reason or cause of the imbalance, in order to nip its potential and accelerated growth in the bud, one must communicate their concerns to the other. It may sound obvious, but in order for the relationship to survive, it's crucial that the discord gets discussed.

Why is it happening in the first place? Because one vibration is beginning to resonate at either a higher or lower rate than the other.

Have you ever wondered how it is that some couples meet in their teens and remain together for the rest of their lives? It's not because they just happened to get lucky. It's because, as they grew and went through life, their frequencies remained together. Of course, that's not to say it was easy…

How many times have you heard people say that you must 'work' at a relationship for it to last? The 'work' part is discussing the discord in order to get the vibrations back to the same frequency. Simple eh?

*'Do what you did in the beginning of a relationship and there won't be an end.'*

*– Tony Robbins*

# The Common Mistake

Let's say you're single and you've now decided you want to be in a relationship. What do you do next? You go on the lookout or the 'hunt' as it were. And how do you do that exactly? Well, it's quite easy isn't it?

All you do is start circulating in all the common areas that similarly single people go. That could be bars, clubs or any form of social gathering. It could also be browsing the Internet and joining one of the many dating sites available. Either way, whichever takes your fancy; it's still a fairly straightforward process. Before you know it, you're out there meeting folk and you're on the dating scene. Excellent.

Unfortunately, this is exactly where the problem of finding your perfect partner lies. It's fine if you're just after a lover or a 'relationship' of some kind or another. But if you truly desire to find the person you're *meant* to be with, then it's unlikely to work.

Now I know what you're thinking. If you can't be 'out there' on the dating scene as it were, then how the hell can you expect to find your perfect partner at all? Well, think of it this way…

Imagine that you're stood in the centre of a large clock. As we know, the clock face is divided into twelve segments. Each segment represents the twelve parts of the process required to find your perfect partner. If twelve o'clock represents the realisation that you've finally met your soulmate, then eleven o'clock denotes the need to first be dating and in the relationship itself.

Herein lies the common mistake that the majority, including myself, have made. Most simply jump straight into the dating scene at eleven o'clock. Straight in at the deep end as it were, crucially missing out ten essential steps.

Why don't we go to one o'clock and work our way round the process? Simply because there hasn't been any instructions, any tuition nor any education about these ten crucial steps . . . until now. In other words, we don't know what we don't know.

It's rather like baking a cake. At eleven o'clock is when it all starts to happen, i.e. placing the ingredients into the oven. However, without following all the steps from one to ten, all you've done is put the wrong ingredients in the wrong tin, into an oven at the wrong temperature: zero. Nothing is going to happen. Or worse still, the oven gets turned on as an afterthought and you end up with a horrible mess.

It's the same with relationships. Most aren't consciously aware of the correct ingredients required to fulfil their desires and expectations. Therefore, unwittingly they miss out steps one to ten and simply end up back in the queue (eleven o'clock) for another seat on the roller coaster ride of rocky relationships.

Of course, those following the recipe will have known that the ingredients were not correct before turning on the oven. This know-how gained from the recipe book, enables them to rectify the issue before it's too late, because they're following the formula. Herein lies the function of this book. To save you time, money and most of all, the horrible mess of unnecessary and painful heartache.

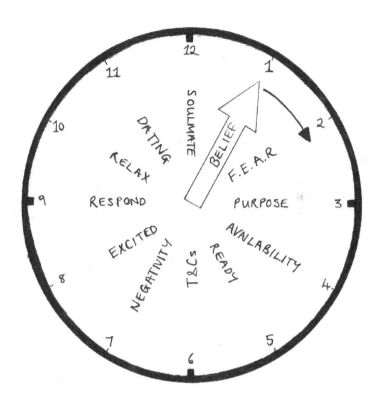

**Around the clock success™**

## Success Route

The procedure or route to success is to simply go from the centre of the clock to number one and naturally follow each step or chapter in turn. Is there a 'fast-track' method? There sure is...

I said at the beginning of this book, that if you're honest with yourself, I guarantee that at least one of the ten reasons will apply to you. There may be more, but will they *all* apply? Probably not. This will be your fast-track.

However, don't mistake a fast-track for a short cut. In other words, keep a firm grip on your integrity as you look yourself in the mirror. Remember, any practise of deception here will ultimately lead to the detriment of one person. You.

Additionally, although you may have recognised that some of the ten reasons were applicable in your past, I doubt they'll all be relevant right now. This doesn't mean that you should ignore them altogether, but rather you become consciously aware of the reasons that, until now, were possibly just unconscious actions.

## Consciously Aware

Becoming consciously aware of our subconscious enables us to focus and direct our intent. As we already know, our intent is our ability to create. And the easiest way to predict the future, is to create it.

"This is all well and good", I hear you say, but exactly how do we become consciously aware of our subconscious? Well, think of it this way; whenever you consciously set an intention, your subconscious immediately gets to work. For example…

Let's say that you need to recall a name. It could be a place, a person or the artist of the song you just heard on the radio. It's on the tip of your tongue and you know you know it, but just can't recall it. You consciously set the intention to recall the name and whilst doing so, your subconscious immediately gets to work in order to help you achieve this.

However, on this occasion your conscious mind fails you and the name isn't recalled from your memory bank. Nonetheless, your subconscious mind continues to search away (although you're not consciously aware of this) and several hours later – BINGO! The name comes to you. Why? Because you never told your subconscious to *stop* working toward your goal. Has this ever happened to you?

Another way to consider this is to think of your mind's memory bank as a filing cabinet. When you wish to recall that name, place or artist of the song, your conscious mind opens the relevant folder from the 'cabinet' and empties the contents onto the table. Everything is now jumbled and it's your subconscious mind that has the task of revealing each of the contents in turn. The name you require may come to you immediately. If not, it will be revealed at a later time, when your subconscious finally reveals it. Again, because you never told it to *stop* working towards your goal.

Your subconscious mind is always at work. In fact, it never rests or stops working towards your intentions and desires.

Just think how quickly you could move towards *any* of your dreams or goals by taking advantage of this simple, yet omnipotent process. By becoming consciously aware and fully focusing on your desires, you will be instructing your subconscious to arrange the conditions necessary to help you achieve your intentions.

Will it take some practice? Of course - new skills are rarely learned overnight. But once you come to believe and *know* that this process really works, you'll begin to function at new heights of self-belief, awareness and understanding.

The conscious mind, when fully focused is all-powerful. The subconscious even more so. Once mastered, a relaxed state of oneness is achieved where no other thought can enter, other than that which is focussed upon. It's beyond relaxation, it's another realm where the *un*conscious mind or 'instinct' takes over...

## Instinct

Watch any sportsman or woman at the top of their game and you will witness this in action. They have a robust, unflappable and single-minded determination to achieve their goal. They also know that trying to force peak performance will not work and can only be achieved intuitively and unconsciously.

The golfer is consciously focused on the hole; it's their unconscious that manufactures the swing. The snooker player is consciously focused on the position of the cue ball *after* he sinks one of the colours. It's the unconscious that manufactures the shot.

Ask a racing driver how they achieve a particularly stunning lap time and often the reply will be that actually, they don't know! This response is pure evidence of the unconscious successfully bringing together all the means necessary to achieve the intention, whilst the conscious mind was focussed on the goal. Nowhere is this better portrayed by the late, great, Ayrton Senna after qualifying in pole position 1.4 seconds ahead of his team mate Alain Prost at the 1988 Monaco Grand Prix...

*"And suddenly I realised that I was no longer driving the car consciously. I was driving it by a kind of instinct, only I was in a different dimension."*

*- Ayrton Senna*

The good news is that this state of achievement is not just available to those at the top of their sport or business. It's accessible to all because we are all capable, worthy and deserving of anything in life that we set our minds to. All that's required is intention, trust and a focussed state of belief that will ultimately take us to a place of *knowing*.

The following illustration helps differentiate between the conscious, subconscious and unconscious mind...

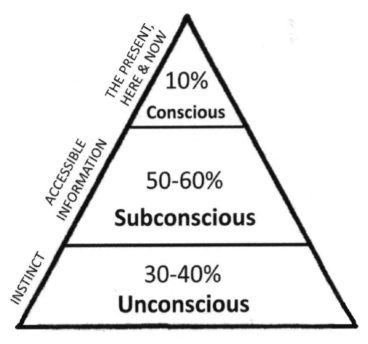

Consciousness of the Human Mind

## Certainty

A question I'm repeatedly asked is: "Do you believe in all this 'stuff'?"

My response is always the same: "No, I don't believe in it. I *know* it."

Can you think of something that you *know* to be the case, while others remain uncertain?

The more you consciously practice becoming aware of your subconscious and unconscious actions, the more your desires will manifest. Little by little will soon become more and more. You will then understand how something can go from seemingly impossible to improbable and then, incredible to inevitable.

It can take the manifestation of the smallest of ambitions, goals or desires to realise the power you possess. It is then that you will *know*. After that, you will become unstoppable in anything you desire to achieve.

Your possibilities and potential are endless, so always remain focused on your dream, purpose or goal. Be unshakable in your belief, trust in the process and the most powerful and amazing results *will* manifest in your life. With practice they'll also be attained instinctively, whilst you remain in a calm state of relaxed unanimity.

The day you become more interested in the awareness of your thoughts, rather than the thoughts themselves, is the day you begin to make things happen.

Make it so.

# AROUND THE CLOCK SUCCESS

In a nutshell:

'Until you make the unconscious conscious, it will direct your life and you will call it fate.'

Carl Jung

'You are a living magnet.
What you attract into your life
is in harmony with your
dominant thoughts.'

Brian Tracy

# 14

# YOUR POWER

In this book, particularly towards the end of most chapters, I have referred to the forces in play that make things happen. In doing so, I have frequently used the words 'energy', 'vibration' and 'frequency'. But what exactly do I mean by this? And what is meant by the need to 'raise' one's vibration or frequency?

Firstly we need to understand what energy is. Energy is literally everything and it's everywhere. Everything is made up of energy; the chair you're sitting on, the clothes you're wearing and even your own body. Yes you and I are made up of it too. Some energy is 'heavier' than others and it's the denseness of the heavier energy that allows our senses to actually see, touch and feel it. Whereas some energy, although we know it's there, we can't see - such as gravity, sound and light waves.

So our bodies are made of energy and we can see them. But can you think of any other forms of energy that we emit, but can't see?

# Connections

Have you ever witnessed an emotional scene, either in real life or maybe whilst watching a film and found yourself getting emotional too? The lump in your throat, or the tear of sadness or joy that you discreetly wipe away can evidence this. Likewise, have you ever seen or heard laughter and again found yourself joining in? Baby laughter is particularly good for this one. Smiling is another good example; have a go at *not* smiling back when you're being smiled at. It's difficult to do.

The emotions, thoughts and feelings we emit, we cannot see, but these are energy too. Energy therefore, is information and all of this information has a vibrational frequency.

For example, think of the sound waves that reach your radio. What happens when you want to change the radio station? You 'tune in' to a different station, which is being emitted at a different frequency. You can't *see* the frequency, but it's definitely there. Just as you couldn't *see* the frequency of the energy being released by that emotional scene. Again, it's definitely there. You know this because you felt it. How and why were you able to feel it? Because it resonated with you and therefore, you were attracted to it.

Likewise, the same applies to music that you hear being played *from* the radio. How is it that some music strikes a chord and appeals to one generation and not another? And why is it that sometimes it's the tune or the beat that holds your attention, whilst other times it's the lyrics? Have you ever lost yourself within a tune or a song and played it over and over again? The answer to all these questions is the same; it's all to do with what resonates.

*"If you want to find the secrets of the universe, think in terms
of energy, frequency and vibration."*

*- Nikola Tesla*

## High or Low?

If all is energy and all energy resonates at differing vibrational
frequencies, what's the difference then between high or low vibrational
frequencies and those that we humans exude, radiate and are able to
project? And, how can we categorise them?

Well thoughts such as kindness, joy, excitement, happiness, gratitude,
abundance, trust, passion and love all have a high vibrational frequency.
Whereas hate, anger, resentment, animosity, bitterness, fear, jealousy,
envy and regret for example, all have a much lower frequency.

Therefore, if you desire to attract a life full of fun, success, positivity,
health, wealth and happiness, which vibrational frequencies do you
think are best suited to resonate with? The higher ones of course.
Conversely, if someone is living a life full of never ending unhappiness,
stress and struggle, which vibrational frequencies are likely to be ever
present in their life? Yes, it's the lower ones. Simple eh?

Here's an example of something I often come across; let's say someone
desires to have more love (high vibrational frequency) in their life,
but they're holding on to bitterness, anger and hatred (low vibrational
frequencies). Do you think they're going to resonate with love if
and when it shows up? Highly unlikely. What's more likely is that
they'll just end up attracting whatever resonates with the existing low
vibrational frequency they're emitting. Remember, what you sow, you

reap and what you send out, you get back. Similarly, like attracts like. So what does bitterness, anger and hatred attract?

Someone expecting to find true love, or for it to find them in these circumstances, is going to be bitterly disappointed. Hardly surprising then, as they were already exuding bitterness in the first place. So can you see how this works?

## Ideals vs Reality

Expecting to find anything on a high vibrational level, whilst holding on to low vibrational emotions, is simply not going to work.

Looking for love in this way is like looking inside that radio for the disc jockey; you know they're there, but you're never going to find them. It's pure fallacy. Those who are unaware of this significance (we don't know what we don't know), continue in their quest, pretending that they're happy, successful and loving people. After all, isn't that what everyone seeks in their partner? Then, oblivious as to the reasons why they can't seem to find love, in time they become disillusioned with what they *do* find (matching low vibrational frequencies). Their frustration can then easily extend to the whole dating scene itself.

Unwittingly, this is where most go wrong. Why? Because we get what we think about the most, whether we want it or not. And the reason we don't attract what we *do* want, is that we attract what we *are*. And what we are is the vibrational attitude or frequency that we emit.

So how do we resolve this mismatch of ideals versus reality? We do so by raising our vibration to match that of the frequency we desire. In other words and as we already know, if we want to receive love, then first we have to be and give love. That's right, just give it away. "Is it really that simple?" I hear you ask. Absolutely. Think of it this way…

## That Which You Are

Have you ever met someone who always seems to exude a high vibrational frequency? Perhaps someone who is always happy, or joyful or positive maybe? The same could be said for anyone who is always kind, thankful or trusting too. These are all high vibrational frequencies and these people are continually attracting what they *are*.

Have you ever been pleasantly surprised when a stranger is kind to you? Waiting and holding a door open for you for example. When this happens, how do you respond? With hatred or with kindness? Most likely with kindness of course. Why? Because you are simply returning that which the stranger gave to you.

Likewise, anyone who exudes low vibrational frequencies does the same. Let's use my friends Kind Kevin and Stressful Steve as examples…

Kevin is a kind (high vibrational frequency) person. One of the ways he shows his kindness is by extending courtesy whilst driving his car. He always allows other vehicles the space to pull out of junctions in front of him. Does Kevin ever have a problem when he needs to pull out of a junction himself? Of course not. His journeys are always relaxed and stress free as the kindness he gave away, is returned to him.

Steve on the other hand, is always stressed (low vibrational frequency) and in a rush when behind the wheel. He never lets others out at junctions, as this will just hinder his journey. Does Steve ever have a problem pulling out of a junction himself? You bet he does! This just compounds his frustration and adds to his stress. And yet, he never understands why this happens to him, whilst the opposite happens to Kevin. Steve feels that this is just another example of the world ganging up on him and he can't figure out what he's done to deserve this or why he's being 'picked on'.

What Steve has yet to realise is this; any low vibrational frequency that he contains, is a poison that only does harm to the container.

When life hasn't flowed so well for you, have you ever felt that the universe was punishing you too? It may have felt like that at the time, but the universe neither blesses nor punishes. It simply responds to that which you *are*.

So, if you find yourself still holding on to any low vibrational frequencies, then unfortunately, this is what you will attract - i.e. nothing but the same. Unless of course, you raise your vibration to match that of your desires. To do this, all you have to do is start reflecting and being that which you wish for. And not just by paying lip service to it either; be it, believe it and become it.

## Mirroring

Is this hard to do when looking for love? Not at all. However, what most people *do* find hard to do is overcome the belief that first they need to give, in order to receive. For example, all too often I hear people say, "I have a lot of love to give", or "Once I find love, I'll be more loving." This approach does not reflect who you *are*, it reflects who you hope to be... one day.

Remember, love is not to be stored up for a rainy day, it's meant to be given away. That way, it will find its way back to you tenfold.

If you've been brought up in a world that taught you to get what you can, whilst you can, or to take whatever you need, when you need it, then yes this may take some overcoming. But hopefully, by now you've read enough for you to concur otherwise. Either way, all you need to do is to start reflecting all that you desire your perfect partner to be…

Do you want someone who is honest and trustworthy? Then *be* honest and trustworthy. Do you want someone who is kind and happy? Then be kind and happy. If you want someone who is loving, be loving. If you want someone to be all of these things, then *be* all of them. You get the picture.

The clever part here, is that you can extend this beyond the aforementioned attributes of who you want your perfect partner to be. What I mean by this is that you have the ability to attract aspects of *where* you want your soulmate to be. This doesn't mean for them to physically be at that party or café, but rather where they are in their life right now. It all descends from the same theme.

## Be First

If you want someone who knows what they want and where they're going in life, then make sure you already do. If you want someone who is available, then make sure you already are. If you want someone who isn't carrying any baggage from the past, then make sure yours is already unpacked. In other words, be there first.

Being first and being consciously aware of the universal laws of attraction, means that you have immense power. You have the ability to make these laws work to your complete advantage and to attract your perfect partner, your soulmate, the one you're here and meant to be with. But in order to do so, you need to add just one more highly influential factor…

In motorsport there's a saying: 'In order to finish first, first you have to finish'. In other words, in order to have any chance of winning, you have to be consistent. The same applies when attracting your perfect partner, i.e. you will need to be consistent in your approach.

Consistency, in this case comes in the form of your belief, your behaviour and your being. With all your heart, consistently be the person you dream of sharing your life with. Don't pay lip service to it, become that person so much, that you can't help but look forward to meeting them.

Now you know how and why this process works, go ahead and make it happen; manifest your magnificent relationship. You *are* more than worthy and fully deserving of such pleasure and happiness.

What's more, your soulmate can't wait to meet you too.

# YOUR POWER
In a nutshell:

'Everything is energy and that's all there is to it. Match the frequency of the reality you want and you cannot help but get that reality. It can be no other way.

This is not philosophy.

This is physics.'

Albert Einstein

'You have two lives.
The second one begins when
you realise you only have one.'

Confucius

# 15

# THE END...
# OF THE BEGINNING

Has this book been entertaining, or has anything you've read made you feel uncomfortable? My hope is both, my preference is the latter. Why? Because the moments that make you feel uncomfortable, are the moments when you learn the most about yourself.

If no nerves have been touched, then no tender truths can be recognised. If no truths are recognised, then no growth is possible. Herein lies this book's objective: To inspire insight, intuition and initiative. In other words, personal development, progression and transformation.

Ah yes, 'change'. That thing that everyone wants but no one wants to do. That thing that pushes you out of your comfort zone and into the unknown. You may occasionally dip your toe into its freezing waters, but more often than not, you step back to the warmth and safety of what you know. But here's the truth about your comfort zone; it's uncomfortable!

# The Uncomfortable Comfort Zone

Once back in your comfort zone, you feel a sense of secure relief. But how long does this last? Over time you become fed up, bored and restless. This can apply to any area of your life: your career, relationships, anything.

The boredom escalates to the point where you become so uncomfortable, that once again, you seek the need for change. Why? Because of the human need for growth. This is why we often attend motivational seminars or pick up self-help books, where we hope we will find the answers we're looking for.

Have you ever done this? If so, how did you feel once you'd left the event or finished reading the book? Elated and enthusiastic that things were now going to be different in your life? If so, how long did that feeling last? Did it fade once you got home from the seminar or put the book back on the shelf? That's not self-development, that's shelf-development! In other words, your library knows more than you do.

Why is it that any excitement, exhilaration or euphoria fails to remain? Is it because you start to be consumed by the pressures of everyday life? No. Nice try, but that's just an excuse. What happens is that the spark, which initially lit the flame in your belly, didn't get fanned enough to turn it into a fire, let alone a furnace.

It's when the fire inside you burns brighter than *any* fire around you that your motivation remains. And when this happens, you become unstoppable. Why? Because now you're driven and not only are you living your life with a sense of purpose, but you're living it *on* purpose.

Remember, having a purpose has everything to do with finding your perfect partner, because people are not attracted to what you do, they're attracted to *why* you do it.

Knowing where you're going in life and why, means you become very attractive indeed. Undeniably, there's nothing more attractive than someone with passion, positivity and purpose. To this end, if you haven't done so already, please apply yourself to the exercises within these pages, if for no other reason than to fan the embers that will constantly fuel your motivation.

## Improvement Begins With I

It is said that when the student is ready, the teacher appears. But the teacher can only tell the student where to look, not what to see. The truth is, nobody knows what's inside you, but you. Only you know what you're made of and in the short time you're here, what you dream of achieving. Nobody else knows.

So tap into your knowing, light the fire in your belly and release your power. The inner power you possess to manifest that which you desire. In this case your perfect partner, your soulmate, the person you're here and *meant* to be with. The only reason this *won't* happen for you, is if you give up your power. And the most common way to give up your power is by believing you don't have any. So what can you do to ensure this doesn't happen to you?

You only require **one** thing to both access and retain your power: Clarity. The clearer you are about what you want, the more certain you are to receive it. Clarity *is* power. Can you think of a time when you were so crystal clear about what you wanted, adamant even, that nothing was going to stop you from getting it? My guess is that you achieved your goal. If you didn't, most likely it was because you stopped believing and gave up your power. And you probably stopped believing because the vision of what you *really* wanted, became blurred and you lost sight of that goal.

Belief and clarity are therefore entwined. Both are high vibrational frequencies that you *will* need to nurture and nourish. This is where and why you must invest in yourself, your growth and your being.

Here is a short, Native American legend that advocates this virtue…

*An old Cherokee is teaching his grandson about life. "A fight is going on inside me." He said to the boy.*

*"It is a terrible fight and it is between two wolves. One is evil; he is anger, envy, sorrow, regret, greed, arrogance, self-pity, guilt, resentment, inferiority, lies, false pride, pretence, superiority, and ego."*

*He continued, "The other is good; he is joy, peace, hope, serenity, humility, kindness, benevolence, empathy, generosity, truth, compassion, faith and love. The same fight is going on inside you, and inside every other person too."*

*The grandson considered this for a minute and then asked his grandfather…* *"Which wolf will win?"*

*The old Cherokee leaned quietly towards him and whispered…*

*"The one you feed."*

# Keep Going, Keep Growing

All the advice in the world will never help or feed you, until you decide to help and feed yourself. And you can't afford not to, if you desire all that you deserve for yourself. That of course includes finding your soulmate - so you'll never regret it either. You already have this book in your hands and yes, you're coming towards the end of it, but that means you're just at the beginning of the best work you'll ever do . . . working on you.

Where you'll be in five years from now depends upon the books you read, the action you take and the people you surround yourself with today. Not everyone around you may be interested in seeing you grow and that's fine. That's more to do with their journey than yours. It's also really important to remember never to allow your ego to get in the way - a poor day for your ego is a rich day for your soul.

What's your purpose? Why are *you* here? Finding what you love to do and sharing it, means you'll never have to 'work' another day in your life.

So nurture, nourish and feed your soul on your journey and converse with those who *raise* your vibration along the way. Invest in yourself, allow your radiance to expand and you will show what is possible for all.

My belief, actually it's my knowing, is that you can achieve anything you desire. My purpose is also crystal clear; to help you align with your soul path, purpose and partner. To this end, if I can ever be of any further service to you via any of my products, live events or personal coaching, I would be most privileged to do so.

I look forward to helping you shine your light.

Your soulmate does too.

# THE END…
# OF THE BEGINNING

In a nutshell:

'Service to others is the rent you pay for your room here on Earth.'

Muhammad Ali

Tony can be contacted at:

www.TheSoulmateSpecialist.co.uk

# ACKNOWLEDGEMENTS

Whilst the making of this book and my story that lies within its pages began many years ago, I can pinpoint two key moments, back in the 1980s, that started me on this journey. It was then I became consciously aware of my thoughts and their power. On both occasions, I was fortuitously, a member of the audience at events facilitated by gentlemen I didn't know personally.

The first was Clive Holmes, founder of the Life Insurance Association (LIA) and later, co-founder of the Institute of Financial Planning (IFP). It was Clive who asked his meditative audience: *"If you knew, really knew you could not fail, what would be the one thing you would do?"* Whilst in my relaxed state, and to my utter astonishment, I wrote down just two words: 'Help others'. Thereafter, this not only had a prolific effect on my approach to anything I did, but has been fundamental in any of my accomplishments. Thank you Clive.

The second was Jack Black, founder of Mindstore. Jack's on-stage presence, energy and teachings had me gripped. I trusted his visualisation techniques and sure enough, manifested exactly what I desired. His power phrase at the time was: *"The greatest gift in life is the ability to have great thoughts and have the strength to take action...*

*whilst others simply dream."* To this day his words are on display in my home. Thank you Jack.

My continued interest in the field of human potential, in the 1990s, led me to a transformational programme called Delfin. This magnificent, metaphysical and magical multi-sensory education was written by Leslie Fieger and facilitated by him and his partner at the time, Sandra Baer (nee Hartley). Delfin took me to new heights of awareness and taught me exactly how and why, what Clive and Jack did, worked. Leslie has kindly contributed the Foreword to this book, but his contribution goes way beyond that. Thank you both, Leslie and Sandra.

We've all experienced difficulties or challenges in our lives and overcoming them has made us who we are today. Likewise, we've all experienced success too. Overcoming a challenge is, in itself, success. Therefore, we all have knowledge and experience of what to do and we all have a story to tell.

However, whilst it's all very well 'knowing' what we know, it's another thing when it comes structuring, articulating and presenting it to others. It's in this area that I give my thanks to Andy Harrington and his Public Speakers Academy. It was there that I was encouraged to dig deep, then deeper still, until I unearthed my 'real' story. Acknowledging the Academy would not be complete without recognising the extraordinary guidance that is Cheryl Chapman.

Whilst knowing who you are and what you have to offer is wonderful, how to then brand and package it to the right audience is the next challenge. This is where my appreciation goes to the experts in this field, Miles Fryer and Sammy Blindell. My gracious thanks to you both, for all you continue to give.

No story would ever exist if it wasn't for the people and personalities who played their part in the making of it. This is why I am grateful to every wonderful woman I've ever met, dated and in some cases, married. Without you and the role you played in my journey, this book would not exist. Thank you.

Inspiration and motivation can come in many forms. My infinite source has always been that of my incredibly grounded, insightful and supportive children, Shelley and Thomas. Thanks guys, I love you both dearly.

My gratitude also extends to the rest of my family and friends who I have no doubt, have at times despaired as to the purpose of where my journey was heading. To be honest, at times I did too.

But most of all, thank you to the light that is my Jeni. I knew I would find you one day and you would be all I ever desired. But never could I have foreseen what we discovered after just six short weeks together. Bless you (and Mr G).

Thank you all.

# RESOURCES

### Chapter 1 – The Cost

*"The amount spent on dating in 2015 rose by a fifth from the previous year, according to an analysis by the Centre of Economics and Business Research. The research, for website Match.com, found the average cost of a date is now £127 for both people, including clothing, gifts, cosmetics, trips to the hairdressers and contraceptives."* Evening Standard, 27th March 2016

http://www.standard.co.uk/news/uk/revealed-the-total-cost-of-the-average-date-as-the-amount-spent-by-single-brits-soars-a3212226.html

*"New research shows that Brits spent more than £5billion looking for romance in 2015 – a whole £1 billion more than they did in 2014. And according to dating firm Match, the average cost for a date, between two people, is £127. This includes the cost of food, drink, cosmetics, gifts, clothes and contraceptives. Research by the Centre for Economics and Business Research found the UK's date-related spending came to £5.16billion,*

*compared to £4.05billion the year before. What we spend it on:- Transport: £10.26, Entertainment, restaurants, bars and pubs: £69.26, Gifts: £6.41, Hairdressers: £7.70, Cosmetics: £5.13, Clothes: £20.52, Contraceptives: £2.57, Eating in: £5.13."* Metro - 27th March 2016

http://metro.co.uk/2016/03/27/this-is-how-much-brits-spend-on-dating-and-its-more-than-the-rest-of-europe-5778090/

*"It typically takes 13 first dates – seven of which will be 'disasters' – before finding 'the one'. Although first dates are expensive affairs, with an average adult investing a total £1,355 on the initial nights out, once the spark is there a further £3,629 is spent on the first year of courtship. The second year in a relationship is significantly cheaper, as the bill for the following 12 months tends to land on £2,760."*

Daily Mail – Mail online - 13th June 2013

http://www.dailymail.co.uk/news/article-2340722/Cost-courtship-Britons-spend-11-000-finding-love-lives.html#comments

*"Research from TopCashback.co.uk… The research of people now in relationships also finds that it took those loved up, on average, 18 months to find that special someone."*

Montrose Review – 13th February 2016

http://www.montrosereview.co.uk/news/the-cost-of-finding-love-1-4027550

*"Death of the seven year itch: Average relationship is now just 2 years and 9 months."*

Daily Mail – Mail Online - 4th February 2014

http://www.dailymail.co.uk/femail/article-2551615/Death-seven-year-itch-Average-relationship-just-2-years-9-months-social-media-blame.html


*"The hidden cost of divorce: New study shows that an average divorcing couple spend £44,000 on their separation – but many spend much more when the hidden costs of starting a new life are factored in."*

The Daily Telegraph - 4th July 2016

http://www.telegraph.co.uk/women/sex/divorce/11041341/The-hidden-cost-of-divorce.html


## Chapter 3 – Belief

*"It also emerged that almost six in ten Brits once reached a point where they felt they were never going to find that special someone. Eight in ten said they met the one when they least expected it, while more than a quarter said their current partner wasn't the type of person they thought they would settle down with. Researchers also found that while 94 per cent of women believe in true love, just 88 per cent of men feel the same way. The statistics emerged in a study commissioned to mark the paperback release today of The Rosie Project, a novel about a man's quest to find his perfect wife."*

Daily Mail - Mail Online – 1st January 2014


http://www.dailymail.co.uk/femail/article-2532213/No-one-said-finding-The-One-easy-The-average-women-kiss-FIFTEEN-men-enjoy-TWO-long-term-relationships-heart-broken-TWICE.html

## Chapter 5 – Purpose

*"Our findings point to the fact that finding a direction for life, and setting overarching goals for what you want to achieve can help you actually live longer, regardless of when you find your purpose," says (Dr) Hill. "So the earlier someone comes to a direction for life, the earlier these protective effects may be able to occur." Previous studies have suggested that finding a purpose in life lowers risk of mortality above and beyond other factors that are known to predict longevity."* APS – Association for Psychological Science – 12th May 2014

http://www.psychologicalscience.org/index.php/news/releases/having-a-sense-of-purpose-in-life-may-add-years-to-your-life.html

*"After being followed for roughly seven years, more than 14,500 of the volunteers died from any cause and 4,000 suffered a heart attack, stroke or other heart-related event. But the researchers found that people reporting a higher sense of purpose in life had a roughly 20 percent lower risk of death during the study period."* News.health.com – 7th December 2015

http://news.health.com/2015/12/07/sense-of-purpose-in-life-may-boost-longevity-heart-health/

*"Most people -- 80% according to Deloitte's Shift Index survey -- are dissatisfied with their jobs."*

Businessinsider.com – 4th October 2010

http://www.businessinsider.com/what-do-you-do-when-you-hate-your-job-2010-10?IR=T

Extracts and interpretations from Sir Ken Robinson's Ted Talk: *"Sir Ken Robinson makes an entertaining and profoundly moving case for creating an education system that nurtures (rather than undermines) creativity."* Ted.com – February 2006 (over 40 million views)

http://www.ted.com/talks/ken_robinson_says_schools_kill_creativity

*"Sir Ken Robinson, PhD is an internationally recognized leader in the development of creativity, innovation and human resources in education and in business."*

http://sirkenrobinson.com/about-2/

*"Adopting a positive mental attitude lowers the risk of suffering a heart attack, requiring surgery and even death. That is according to a new study by a group of scientists at University College London. The research found after suffering a heart attack or angina, the most pessimistic patients were twice as likely to suffer a more serious health condition in the next four years, compared with the most optimistic patients."* Daily Mail - MailOnline – 5th March 2015

http://www.dailymail.co.uk/health/article-2980770/It-s-true-Optimists-live-longer-Having-positive-attitude-lowers-risk-heart-attack.html

## Chapter 13 – Around the Clock Success

*"The Conscious, Subconscious, And Unconscious Mind – How Does It All Work?"*

The Mind Unleashed – 13th March 2014

http://themindunleashed.org/2014/03/conscious-subconscious-unconscious-mind-work.html


*"Three Minds: Consciousness, Subconscious, and Unconscious"*
StarOverSky Counseling & Psychotherapy - 23rd May 2013

https://staroversky.com/blog/three-minds-conscious-subcosncious-unconscious

# NOTES

# NOTES

# NOTES